Tales of
along

Home

**Conversations with people who are 'dead',
but don't know it yet ...**

By Paul E Moss

This book provides evidence on what it truly
means to '*die*', as told by the *real experts*,
those who are '*dead*'. They will tell *stories to
make your heart sing,* via a dedicated team of
trance-mediums, conduits for Spirit.

*Unveiling the great mystery,
shining light on the transition
and easing grieving.*

Contents

Bible quote reference:
THE HOLY BIBLE, NEW INTERNATIONAL
VERSION®, NIV® Copyright © 1973, 1978, 1984, 2011
by Biblica, Inc.® Used by permission. All rights reserved
worldwide.

References

*This book is mainly based on the work of the Salumet
Circle.*
*All Spirit rescues included have the actual audio
recordings freely available on the website: You can
find all the Spirit rescue audios and much more here:*

**www.salumetandfriends.org/rescue-
work/book-rescues/**

Others mentioned:
*Carlos Castaneda – 'Journey to Ixtlan - The lessons
of Don Juan' – Penguin Books - 1973*
*Colin Wilson - 'C. G Jung Lord of the Underworld' -
The Aquarian Press - 1984*
*Louise Hay – 'You can Heal your life' – Hay House
1984*
*THE HOLY BIBLE, NEW INTERNATIONAL
VERSION*

David and Zoe Sulem - 'God's plan for All' - CreateSpace Independent Publishing Platform - 2017/12/11

J.K.Rowling 'Harry Potter and the Deathly Hallows' – Bloomsbury publishing – 2007

Charles Dickens – A Christmas Carol – 1843

The two worlds of Helen Duncan, by Gena Breasley – Regency press 1985

Estelle Roberts – 50 years a medium: the autobiography of Estelle Roberts - SDU Publications (20 Sept. 2006)

The *Salumet transcripts* are *freely available* and can be read from the beginning, in one *large PDF:*

www.salumetandfriends.org/app/download/ 12318576/Salumet+-+All+Trascripts+94+- +May+2023.pdf

Useful links: ✈

We're not on FB, Tik-Tok, X, Instagram, Telegram or the telephone etc. but we have 2 websites!

www.salumetandfriends.org *–A chronologically organised Library of transcripts, audios and other trance-channellings, since the first Salumet communication on 27th June 1994.*

www.salumet.org *–An A-Z of the teachings, arranged by subjects, allowing quicker access to the material.*

There are also several books, featuring the teachings of Salumet:

'Salumet: His Mission to Planet Earth' ...you are already on the pathway of Light. 2005 – George E Moss

'The Chronicles of Aerah' – Mind-Link Communications across the Universe. 2009 – George E Moss

'Earth's Cosmic Ascendancy' – Spirit and Extraterrestrials guide us through Times of Change and Challenge. 2014 – George E Moss

'The Aether' - Cradle of Creation and Vital to All Life. 2023 – George E Moss (To be published by Christmas 2023)

And also ...

'A Smudge in Time'. 2000 – George E Moss. George's first book, aimed at scholars of history and science, with input from Salumet.

Foreword

This compilation of words will hopefully give readers a realisation of how Love and Truth exist.
The author has been a dedicated worker for Spirit, as have many others, including myself.
The words given to us are always simple, yet so powerful.
So, take what you can from them and go forward, with the knowledge that we have been given, to others.

> *Eileen Roper*—full-trance medium for *Salumet.*

"If that powerful interest that you all show to things outside your planet, if that interest were to be turned *inwards*, in understanding the *vehicle* which you all inhabit, dear friends what a powerful force that would be. When understanding, when knowledge is sought, when all that you wish and desire is turned towards knowing the self, then indeed are you beginning to know what you are about. Friends, when that happens, all that lies beyond your understanding at this time would belong to you in an instant. No longer would your skies be a mystery to you, because then, dear friends, you would be *part* of it, you would become a *living force* within it; no longer would your skies seem to be a miracle, but become part of your very *existence.* So friends, listen to me, turn your thinking *inward* to the very depths of your understanding, reach out for that knowledge — and it is innate within you all, have no doubts about that and find the mystery *within.* Seek that dear friends and you will find all—If you are not prepared to *seek* and to *search,* then you will not *find.*

These simple words I have given to you this time are the most important ones that I can say to you. *Find* your *true self* and all of the cosmos will fall into place.

There is no reason why in this lifetime, you could not attain this. So, to you all I say: *SEEK, ASK, FIND* — it is there for you, if only you should *take up* — shall I call it, a *challenge?* I would say to you: As you look towards the stars and planets in your skies, look inwards to yourself and find that *eternal flame* which you are, because dear friend, you are brighter than the brightest star—you have to visualise this first."

Salumet 1997/04/14

Acknowledgements

Deepest thanks to the *very dedicated* team, past and present, of what has come to be known as the *'Salumet Circle'*, based in England. This circle, which is truly a *spiritual family*, has its counterparts in *Spirit realm*, including *gatekeepers, guides, helpers* and others of whom we may not even be aware. My heart is full with *gratitude and Love* to *all*, both *here* and in *Spirit realm*. I pray that this book in some way does justice to all those involved in this *Labour of Love.*

Thank you!

Thank you!

Introduction

*O*nce upon a time, in a land far, far away….

Many believe that there are no *chance events* and that everything is *orchestrated* by a higher force, nudging us along certain pathways. It is now clear that *'guiding nudges'* brought together a *synergistic group of people*, forming what became known as the *Salumet Circle.* Here's a quick look at key events, which opened doors to this *new world:*

I'd been backpacking in Central America in 1989, with my brother Mark, inspired by *Carlos Castaneda's* books, searching for something *'real'*, in a world full of illusion, pollution, hypocrisy, inequality/greed, wars—the darker side of life, with so many conflicting emotions and confusion spinning around in the mind.

I'd just finished a *Psychology degree*, but that didn't answer the *deeper questions* and part of this trip was about searching for *Truth* and finding *direction*—a way through all the contradictions and *chaos*. I lacked knowledge and understanding and had my fair share of *fears,* but I knew I needed to *learn*.

While enjoying a cuppa in the *Magic Flute café,* in San Christabel, Mexico, we met a woman describing herself as an *'energy healer'*—I didn't know what that meant, but meeting her was *cathartic*—It felt exciting, self-empowering and she got me started on *more harmonious living, meditation* and gave an important message: **'When you return to England, you will need 'Trance-Mediums' to keep you on the right path.'**

I began to feel reawakened, stopped eating meat and started to meditate as a daily routine. I loved *(and still do)* this simple yet deep way of connecting to Spirit, with no *'middle-men'*—just *YOU* and *SPIRIT* communing together, *'plugging in'* to *Source.*

The pyramids of Central America provided a beautiful landscape, offering *long meditative walks* through jungles pulsating with the sounds of crickets, birds, monkeys—nature's orchestra of *life.* I would stop to rest under giant trees, and practice being 'still'*,* because only the *still mind* can truly *'listen'* to the *Spirit within.*

In practising those tricky steps of *quietening* the mind and slowing the *internal dialogue,* there's the feeling of opening up to deeper **Love**—but there's still that mischievous *monkey-mind*, yapping on about what else there is to do, instead of *'wasting time'* learning meditation… *maybe try it tomorrow*, *next week*, *next year* … everyone has different monkey mischief—same-same, but different …

The deep breathing and relaxation brought a real sense of *p e a c e*—gradually calming, clearing the busy/*buzzy* mind and these *boundless feelings* eventually outshine all the monkey-business—but one *little monkey* still had some *business* with me: Whilst gently *coming out* of meditation, I slowly opened my eyes to the delightful site of a monkey far away on the floor of the jungle. This was exciting, because I'd only ever seen monkeys high above in the canopy of the giant trees, never on the ground—and this one was moving towards me!

I remained as still as I could, gently breathing, eyes fixed ahead, as the monkey continued its leisurely stroll in my direction. I stayed as motionless as possible, which is easier to do when practising the stillness and peace of meditation. In spite of the stillness, there was also of course, growing excitement, and the closer the monkey got, the more my excitement *grew*. I anticipated that as it got closer and closer, it would surely see or sense me, but intriguingly it continued its leisurely advance, until it was perhaps *10 meters* away. By now, in spite of the meditative state, my young heart was *quickening*— and *still it kept coming!* 5 meters and my eyes must have been popping out. But it just kept approaching, continuing its unrushed stroll: 3 meters, 2 meters, 1 meter and then, in amazement, it *climbed onto my lap* and put its *arms around me!*

I was stunned, but perhaps thanks to a new-found inner peace, I found my arms embracing my new friend.

Time stood still, as we embraced for this *magical-monkey-moment*, before the monkey's long arms began to loosen, which I took as a sign to release the hug, and the monkey continued its journey, leaving me in teary-eyed *wonderment.*

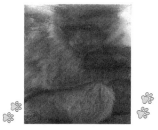

Everything *is interconnected*—in Physics jargon there's '*Unified field*' and '*Quantum Entanglement*', where *all particles* are *connected* and cannot be described *independently* regardless of *distance*—they are part of *One Whole...* So, achieving a peaceful meditative state *will* permeate surrounding atmosphere--animals, plants, people, monkeys and all Creation in some way *'senses' change* and reflects it. This is why *real* change begins *within*, as we raise our *thought vibrations*, expanding the *Love* energy, *inviting change* first within ourselves and then *rippling out* into the *beautiful world. Confucius* talks about putting your own house in order first and then the country changes. Meditation is like a doorway to *Source,* a way to tune into *deeper Love*, facilitating *real* change from the *heart.*

"You must begin somewhere, yes. It is an exercise which must be done if you wish to raise that consciousness to that which is your very *selves.* **I would say to you, it is a very** *individual* **thing. You cannot be guided by another, only in the** *elementary stages.* **But I say to you** *all***, find that element, which you find is** *LOVE***, and focus upon**

12

that area. It may be, as you have spoken upon, beautiful singing, if that is your heart's desire. Many have found the peace and stillness, within the background of beautiful music. *(For)* others, this would be too intrusive, so I say to you all, find that quietness and stillness, which suits you best. Sometimes it is better to, say, focus your attentions upon the flame of a candle. This serves more than one purpose. With this exercise, I can say to you, so too would the use and development of your *'auric vision'* be expanded. For another, it may just be that they focus upon something as simple as one of your beautiful earthly flowers. I say, find your own *thing*. Do not be concerned, if at first you find, not very much happens, this is *not* to be worried about. Take it slowly, *slowly* and you will find that that consciousness *will* be raised. You see, once you begin to meditate, then you have *control* over your everyday thoughts …"

Salumet 1994/11/28

(More information on meditation in Appendix 2)

After a wanderlust trip through Central America, full of synchronicities and a few feisty tummy upsets, it felt like there was a meaningful pathway and though I was socially still a *shy English nitwit*, this trip was a *guiding light!*

Returning to the magical old *United Kingdom*, overflowing with ancient history, like the warrior queen *Boudicca* who *fought for freedom* against the oppressive Roman empire, intent on *crushing* so-called *'witches'*—the *healers* and *wise-ones* possessing *unique spiritual gifts*—replacing them with *drone-like* priests, *imposing patriarchal* systems, *shackling* people in *chains of fear*. And then there was *Merlin* and *King Arthur! But I digress…*

I was *home*, bubbling from a *magical trip*, where I'd been given guidance: **'I would need to find trance-mediums…'**—so this was my main focus and within a couple of weeks, thanks to *divine timing/nudges*, I met a lady who was part of a weekly circle, involving trance-work/mediums—and a new *door opened...*

I didn't know what to expect, but as we parked outside the bungalow, *number 6, Love Lane*, all seemed pretty *ordinary*. I was greeted by *Leslie Bone*, an elder, dapperly-dressed gentleman, with penetrating eyes and a squinty smile from behind half-moon glasses. I understood quickly, that Mr Bone was a no-nonsense guy. He had been doing this work for many years and for him, it was all about *BEING of SERVICE sincerely* to *GREAT SPIRIT*. The emphasis was *keeping it simple*. Over the years, *Leslie* had been guided by *Spirit* about what was needed and what was unnecessary. *(Les regarded unnecessary stuff as distractions.)* Meetings would often begin with a little meditative music, sitting comfortably in silence, with minimal lighting, offering ourselves to be of *Service to Spirit*, in *Truth* and *Love*, asking for the protection of *Great Spirit*. If specific arrangements were needed, *Spirit* would instruct. I liked this aspect of Leslie's circle, because it seemed to reduce the possibility of *ego-interference*—we were led humbly by what *came*

14

from *Spirit*, via the *trance-mediums.* Most of '*me*', wanted to believe, but there was also the *sceptic*, the *academic/psychology graduate*, who had a hard time '*letting go*' and trusting *feelings.*

One thing *was clear,* these were *genuine people*, who *truly believed* in what they were doing; and like me, all had gravitated there by *word-of-mouth*, guided by '*chance*' meetings. My *sceptical aspect* had to accept that all was *freely given*—but what really surpassed everything else, was the simple fact that at *every meeting* there was a *homely sense* of *Peace* and *Love.* Spirit was *powerful* and yet *gentle* and it just felt '*right*' being there—a new stage of *cosmic education* was beginning...

"You must collect all information, collate it and then take only what *you* can accept at the time. We ask nothing else of you and I have told you also, if any of my words are unacceptable to you, then you reject them, because of course, that *is* your freewill, and that is part of the understanding of *Spirit.* That is part of your own *growth.*"

Salumet 2005/06/13

Chapter 1

Afterlife Myths

*W*e ask ***Oh Great Creative Force***, help us to control our wayward senses, help us to know the player of them, help us to control fear with hope, despair with joy, sadness with happiness. Help us to gather that power and light within us that we may go forward, to help all of mankind. Of these things, we ask help and encouragement and Light.

Salumet 1997/09/01

Research suggests that most people believe life continues after *'death'*, though the exact nature of the *afterlife* is confused and riddled with fears. With something as inevitable as *death*, a clearer understanding is desirable, which may help navigate this *earthly voyage*. Much like when ancient man feared thunderstorms until it was understood that it wasn't the wrath of the Gods, but part of an amazing **weather-cycle**, similarly we may come to see *'death'* as part of a miraculous *physical-spiritual* **life-cycle**. Fears about disembarking the *Earth-plane*, with a one-way ticket to a punitive realm, tormented by a sadistic, goatee-guy, waving a fork, sounds like a *preposterous fantasy*. There are parallels in other faiths, though Christianity seems most unbending, considering it to be *'eternal damnation'*—zero opportunity for redemption.

World religions provide *important frameworks* and many gain great comfort from them and this chapter is *not* about trying to undermine *beautiful teachings*, but a little closer study can lead to clearer understanding, which after all, is the main purpose of such teachings, to provide greater understanding, so that we can more fully comprehend, embrace and honour the teachings.

'Grave' misconceptions:

There are 4 *distinct words* in the Bible, each translated as 'Hell': **'Sheol'** actually means *'the grave'*, or *'the pit'*. **'Hades'** and **'Tartarus'** originate from *Greek* mythology and **'Gehenna'** is a valley in Jerusalem. *'Gehenna'* was the word most used by *Jesus* and some background context may be of interest: In those days the *Gehenna valley* was used as the *city dump*, with a constant fire burning rubbish. Clearly, Jesus was referring to the *local* rubbish fire *down in the valley*, *NOT* some *'other-worldly'* realm of *eternal damnation*, with that red-horned plonker. As you'll see below, the whole story of the Devil in *Hell* hadn't even been conceived of yet, suggesting all of those different words for Hell *when originally used*, conveyed other meanings:

The Devil is NOT in the 'detail'—dumped in Gehenna?

Speaking of the devil, this is a *medieval biblical embellishment.* Lucifer, originally meant *'Morning Star'* or *'Lightbringer'*, another word for *Planet Venus.* Over time, Lucifer got *rebranded* as the *'devil'*, influenced greatly by medieval *fantasy books!* Borrowing from the work of *fictional writers such as* Dante, and Milton, who created entertaining *tales* about Lucifer *'falling from grace'* and becoming *Satan* in a *scary, fantasy world* called *'Hell' (Not to be confused with the Gehenna valley dump!)* The popularity of their stories didn't go *unnoticed* and some of them ended up in *Christian teachings!* Alas, if copyrights had existed back then, it may have been a different *story/myth* ...

Similarly, Beelzebub, *(aka Lord of the flies)* is a name derived from the Canaanite God *Baal.* These 'Gods' of indigenous peoples were seen as *enemies or competitors* and labelled *'Baddies'.* Baal was actually the *God* of *fertility*, *not* a mumbo-jumbo *'demon'.* The *demonisation* of *Gods of fertility*, *Goddesses* and the *feminine*, somehow *'justified'* blanket inequality, *male-only priesthoods* and unholy witch-hunts. The truth is, so-called *'witches'* and *'demons'* were a form of propaganda—medieval mechanisms of control. *'Demon'* stems from the word *'deity'*... There *are* dark/negative entities, but nothing *'evil'* as such. *Pure Love* has no equal. There is only *Pure Love* versus the **darkest fear**, which is confused/tainted *Love* that when finally healed, returns back to *LOVE.* All *Creation* has a divine *Spark* of *Love* within, even though it can be *buried deeply—more on that later...*

18

So, the concept of *'Hell'* is entangled in *mistranslations* and the *Satan/devil* saga, which is a medieval *embellishment*—the word *'evil'*, is derived from *'devil'* and is therefore equally misleading. When you *think* about it, if God is *Good/Pure Love*, then it makes sense that *Love* is the only *real Power/energy*. Why would a *God of Love* conceive of *'eternal damnation' with* zero chance of redemption? The true opposite of *Love* is *fear,* which *disconnects* people from Source/God/Love. We are never fully disconnected, but with *'poor connection/signal strength'*, we don't get to *hear* our inner guidance and can become spiritually *lost.*

There is of course *great wisdom* in the Bible and many in the church *are* aware of *mistranslations and meddling* and do their best within their *spheres* of *influence.* So, not wishing to *quibble* about *Biblical boo-boos*—there's no blame, it's all part of the learning and if we replaced those notions of **'devil'** and **'evil',** with more friendly/digestible terms like **'ego/selfishness'** and **'ignorance/unawareness'**, we'd have a closer understanding of the original meanings. It's time the Bible had a *proper 'make-over'* with *all mistranslations* and *embellishments* corrected. Then the beautiful *core Love teachings* would *shine forth* even more strongly, no longer tainted with *fear* and *hocus-pocus.*

Salumet dismisses Hellfire:

"Firstly, let me say about visions and words that are uttered in the name of religions. You know, my dear friends, when first I came to you, I came to

you with words of *Truth* and *Love*—I also told you that many would not accept these words—and that you have found to be true also. You must remember that different religions have their own tenets of belief. The words used at *Fatima* are those from religion that you now call *'Catholicism'*—and they preach that there is *'hellfire'*, which I have to say is —and I do *not* apologise for such *strong words*—but it is all *NONSENSE.* It has been spoken at a time when people were not literate—not the recent visitation, but the previous beginning of that religion. It was to hold the people in a grip that they could not free themselves from. It was a teaching of *'fear'*, and this the gentleman must try to understand. I am here to tell him, there is no such thing as *'Hell'*, in the sense that he recognises it. No-one person remains separated from the Love of that Great Spirit for all time. Everyone who passes into Spirit, is cared for and loved—even those who have wronged themselves in any lifetime, are *never* forgotten. The gentleman needs to recognise that any 'hellfire feelings' are feelings of their own worth. No-one punishes you except yourself."

Salumet 2013/07/15

Chapter 2

Rescue Work and Being of Service

⊥

*W*hen you return *HOME*, you of course *are Spirit.* On Earth you are cloaked in this garb of flesh: You are *not physical beings* with a *Spirit*, you are *Spirit* with a *cloak* of *human flesh.*

Salumet 2007/09/24

The Salumet Circle, is nothing to do with church, religion or any mystic *'ism'*—we are simply a group of everyday people who meditate and do *trance-work*, as a way to be of *Service* to *Great Spirit/God/Creation*. During the meetings there are sometimes **'Spirit rescues'**, involving people who have *'died'*, but due to fear or confusion, do not transition to Spirit world, Heaven, Nirvana, Jannah, Paradise, Xanadu or whatever term you wish. When people do not transition to the *afterlife*, their *non-physical Spirit* can be brought to *rescue circles*, where clear communication via trance-mediums is given to explain the situation.

If left alone, the now *nonphysical* person will linger in confusion, perhaps getting upset when others move into *'their'* property—objections of course go *unheard,* as they are no longer *Physical.* This is one explanation for *ghost hauntings*, where an *uneasy presence* is *sensed*, which is usually a previous inhabitant, confused and unhappy that strangers have moved into *'their'* house! So, *rescue work* is like *'ghost clearing',* where *'dead' (non-physical)* people are encouraged to move on to *Spirit world*, our true *HOME.*

Spirit rescues have many similarities with research obtained from *Near Death Experiences (NDEs),* which also typically involve moving through a *Tunnel of Light*, reunification with loved ones and *tremendous feelings* of *Love* and *Peace.* The main difference is that with *rescues,* the *physical body* is finished, so the *Tunnel of Light* is a *one-way ticket—* they do not return to the *earthly life*, but take on an *etheric body,* like a new *avatar. (More on that later.)* Contemplating the fact that we have *limited time* here, can bring sobriety and wisdom—this is supported by *NDEs*, which give a glimpse into the deeper nature and purpose of life. The Psychologist *Carl Jung*, had a *life-changing NDE* at the age of 68, providing the knowledge and motivation to *break free* from doctrinal, *'follow-the-sheep'* science and begin his *greatest works*, thanks to his *life-changing NDE.* The rescues chronicled here may also be insightful and much like *Carl Jung*, we may also *swim* in waters of *deeper understanding.*

There are other methods to accomplish the same thing, such as when *Psychics* visit the *location* of someone who has *'died',* but has not *'transitioned'* yet. Through *psychic* communication with the *'dead person'*, they can similarly be encouraged to move onwards into the *Light*, without the need of a *Spirit rescue group.* This is another way of performing the same task, which can be done by individuals who possess the sensitivity, inner strength and knowledge. All the *rescues* included here, take place within the walls of a weekly meeting house. The *'dead people'* are brought to the group via *gatekeepers* and other helpers in *Spirit world*, using *trance-mediums*, who act as conduits—the *voice box* of the *medium is 'borrowed'* by the one being *rescued*, allowing the whole group to hear and participate, giving a further level of protection. It may sound complicated, but it *will* become clear in the next chapter, where transcripts are presented, illustrating what this work is all about and the audio recordings of the actual rescues are available here:

www.salumetandfriends.org/rescue-work/book-rescues/

We are also tremendously blessed to have *Salumet*, *channelled* through Eileen, a *full-trance* medium. *(Eileen is unconscious when Salumet speaks, preventing any ego-interference.)* Salumet is a ***'conglomerate being'***, a *union of many*, like a *'Universe of knowledge'* not confined to this little earthly planet, in the *back-waters* of the *Milky Way.*

The *words* may *resonate*, because they are *spiritual truths* echoed by many throughout history. *'TRUTH'* just *'IS'*, whether it comes from *ancient scriptures, Jesus, Mahamed, the Buddha, Confucius, Guru Nanak,* **Yoda ...**

Salumet adds a *special touch of Unconditional Love:*

"**Those of us in our world do not abandon those Spirits who you would term,** *'evil'.* **I have spoken to you before that each individual Soul, has a** *Spark of Divinity* **within it, which can be helped along. It may take aeons of time, but it is not abandoned, it is** *showered with Love,* **until such time as the recognition of its own actions become known to it. It would be so much easier, if that Love was given and expanded to** *all* **those peoples, whether** *politicians,* **whether** *ordinary peoples,* **who** *need* **help, to** *Lighten* **your world. It would be much better that they received help whilst within the** *physical body.* **So my friends, open up your hearts to all those who I know some of you would find difficult to accept into your prayers, but you would be blessed indeed, if you were so to do this. Those who work within these spheres of work, with these poor Souls—and you must try to see them in that way—again we come back to judging your fellow man. However** *'evil'* **they have been, they still are** *Sparks* **of that** *Great Creative Divinity.* **All eventually must return to the** *Light*—**I am moving now into deep, deep matters. All, all energies must return from whence they came, if it takes aeons of time, so be it. But never,**

24

never, never, will one Soul be left alone; it will be helped, it will be surrounded by *Love*, until such time as the Soul can move forward."

Salumet 1996/01/29

Now, let's ***dive*** into the *Spirit Rescues*!

 *Yippee!*

Chapter 3

Love-bonds

W*hen we* bring to you rescues, it is because the *Spirit* has shown a glimmer of light in the way Spirit is thinking, but because it has been encased within the darkness of its thoughts, it is closer to your world sometimes. Therefore, we need *your* help and the easiest way if that individual Spirit will not listen entirely to us, or one who has gone before, is to return it through a medium, who the Spirit normally will accept, although not always, but it allows that Spirit to think about what has been said to them.

Salumet 2005/09/05

All meetings have been dedicatedly *recorded and transcribed* throughout the last *30 years*, so you may wish to visit the website to listen to the *actual voices* in addition to reading the transcripts. This is *not Hollywood,* these are *real life/death* rescues of *people* speaking through *trance-mediums. (Audio links[1] and transcripts are presented in full, except in rare instances, where there is minimal editing to respect privacy.)*

---

[1] Listen to audios here: www.salumetandfriends.org/rescue-work/book-rescues/

The first rescue *(2015/11/02)* begins with a lady angry that Lilian had entered her house. Sometimes the transition we call *'death',* goes unnoticed—this lady simply didn't realise she had *'died'* and was no longer in her *PHYSICAL body*—she was talking to Lilian via the *trance-medium* Eileen. So-called *'ghosts'*, are often just *people* who are stuck and need a little help by people like Lilian and others:

Lilian: Hello. *(Pause)* Do you wish to talk? *(No.)* Feeling a bit cross? *(Yes.)* Well, it might help if you could talk about it—sharing it with someone helps sometimes.
I didn't let you in.
Lilian: Well, I crept in, but I'm quite friendly.
You don't go creeping into people's places!
Lilian: Well, I think I've crept in to help you.
Where's my stick?
Lilian: How many sticks do you have, one or two, to help you walk around?
I don't believe this—walking into my house—who do you suppose you are?
Lilian: Well, I'm here to help—that's the thing you need to remember. If you could tell me your—
Are you that new nurse they promised me—they promised me, they did.
Lilian: I'm just someone to help you.
Do what?
Lilian: Well, to show you—or at least to tell you what's happened and why I'm here. Did you feel unwell all of a sudden?
I'm always unwell dear.

27

Lilian: But did you feel even more—a little bit faint perhaps? *(Yes.)* You closed your eyes?

Just for a second—but I'm fine now, you can see I am.

Lilian: Yes, I know you're fine now. But had you ever thought what would happen when you died?

Of course.

Lilian: What did you think?

Well, they'd bury me.

Lilian: And that would be the end of that? *(Yes.)* Right—well it's not the end, in fact it's a new beginning, and that's the bit that you hadn't thought about. I'm just here to tell you that we *live on.*

No—that's a lot of tosh!

Lilian: Well, you feel perfectly well?

Yes, I'm fine.

Lilian: Yes, you feel nice and warm, and do you feel a lot of love around you? Think about it—you feel a pull towards love? And that seems to be pulling you forward—you feel happy.

I feel—yes, I suppose I do—yes, I suppose I do, in a way.

Lilian: And ahead of you, you can see light?

I can't see anything.

Lilian: Well, you just wait a little while and you'll see a light—a light that will draw you to it. And you'll see someone waiting, and that someone is waiting to take you forward into Spirit. Although you hadn't thought about it, it's there and we all have to go the same way, to start a new life.

This is too much to take in.

28

Lilian: It is, I understand—if you hadn't thought about it, it's just a bit too much, but it will make sense to you as you move forward. *(Oh!)* Who can you see?

Like a little star—pretty little star—mm.

Lilian: Getting bigger?

Mm, yes—I'm really confused now.

Lilian: Try not to be confused, but what can you see in the light? —in the star?

It's like sunshine—big rays of sunshine, and it's almost...

Lilian: Who would you like to see that has passed on before you?

Well, I don't want to see that husband of mine.

Lilian: No, well we'll forget him then.

I didn't have any children.

Lilian: No—did you have a pet, a pet dog or cat?

I had a cat.

Lilian: Would you like to see the cat again?

Oh—not too bothered. (Pause) Oh yes! It's my good friend from years and years and years ago! I should have married him!

Lilian: Oh! Now you can be friends and have a good old chat about days gone by.

Well, well! He looks like a young man!

Lilian: And that's what you'll look like quite quickly.

A young man?

Lilian: No, but you'll feel a lot better; as long as you go forward—that's the main thing. I've done my job then.

I have to move forward...

Lilian: Yeah, towards your friend.

Well, it's like he's coming to get me. (Good) *Well—do you know something?*

<u>Lilian</u>: A nice surprise?

No—I LIKE you!

<u>Lilian</u>: *(With a chuckle)* Good.

Oh, this is lovely!

<u>Lilian</u>: Yes, the main thing is you've listened to me and that's all that matters.

I never would have believed it could be so lovely, and I'm not in that old chair anymore, am I?

<u>Lilian</u>: No, you won't need it.

I'm free, I'm free, yes, I'm free!

<u>Lilian</u>: And you're happy to go—I'm sure you are.

Bye—goodbye.

<u>Lilian</u>: Bye.

Love-bonds remain strong after so-called *'death'*, which is just a *new beginning...*

This next rescue *(2013/07/29)* is another example of someone not realising their *physical body* had *'expired',* which is why no-one could see or hear her, perhaps just sensing an *'uneasy presence'.* When rescues are performed, all this is *cleared.*

Another *type* of *'ghost',* is where *'energy imprints'* are left in the *ether* for reasons not fully understood—

it is a *residual energy* which fades in time, though may remain for *hundreds of* years. There are also *'visitations'* from loved ones, who of course don't need *rescuing*, because they have made their transition and are simply returning because the *love-bond always remains. ('Ghosts' is just an umbrella term, but mostly we are talking about non-physical beings.)*

Lilian: Good evening—welcome.

Could you direct me to Miss Shelbourne please? I believe I've lost my way.

Lilian: Where were you going?

To see Miss Shelbourne. Why can you hear me and the others can't?

Lilian: Yes, I see. I've got some explaining to do for you.

No, I don't need any explanations, I just need to find Miss Shelbourne.

Lilian: You were going to see Miss Shelbourne?

Yes—I must have lost my way.

Lilian: Were you walking? *(Yes.)* Did you feel unwell at all? *(No.)* That may seem a strange question—a headache maybe?

Well, a little indigestion perhaps—that's all, nothing to concern myself about.

Lilian: Well, did you ever wonder what would happen if you suddenly died?

Oh, my goodness, what a strange question!

Lilian: What would happen—where you would go?

Well, of course!

Lilian: Where do you think you would go?

I would hope I would go to Heaven.

Lilian: Yes, well you are on your way to Heaven. I think that indigestion that you felt, turned into a heart-attack, and I'm sorry to bring you the shock of this.

That's a very great shock!

Lilian: Yes of course, and that's why you couldn't get people to know that you were there.

I did think they were very rude.

(When the physical body dies, the transition to the etheric body can go unnoticed.)

Lilian: Yes, that's because it was your *spiritual self*, and that's what you are now—as real as the other one.

My spiritual self— well, well!

Lilian: You feel well and light?

I don't feel any different!

Lilian: No, you won't.

But surely, I would know—surely, I would know if I had died?

Lilian: If you have a sudden heart-attack, or maybe a sudden stroke, it is a shock. If people are killed on the road or in any way that's sudden, it's a shock and unfortunately, this is what happened to you.

So, I'm in shock?

Lilian: Yeah, you were, but you'll be okay.

So, where's dear Miss Shelbourne? Am I not to see her? Am I to just let things go?

Lilian: She will already know that you've passed into Spirit—she will already know that. If you think about it, your body would have been found.

I see—this is very confusing.

Lilian: So really, you're on your way to Heaven.

On my way… are there no steps?

<u>Lilian:</u> No, I don't think there are any steps. What you should be looking for to begin with, is a light—a bright light ahead of you.

And what will be in the light?

<u>Lilian:</u> Someone waiting for you. Who would you like to meet you? Who has already gone before you?

Well, I'm quite loathe to tell you.

<u>Lilian:</u> You don't have to tell me.

I—d'you know, I never married, but I did have a beau who died very young.

<u>Lilian:</u> Well good for you. Maybe it will be *him* waiting. I hope so.

That would be pleasant.

<u>Lilian:</u> Wouldn't it just!

Do you think he would remember me?

<u>Lilian:</u> Oh, without a doubt.

But I look so different.

<u>Lilian:</u> Well, that wouldn't make any difference; he'll see you spiritually now.

Well—I really don't know much about this 'Spirit'.

<u>Lilian:</u> As long as you believe in Heaven, your Spirit goes to Heaven.

(Even if you don't believe in 'Heaven/Spirit realm', it's where we all go.)

I do, and I have to say: I feel rather comfortable now—not at all worried about Miss Shelbourne.

<u>Lilian:</u> Good—she'll be fine. *(Yes)* She may already be there. But she'll know what happened to you, so I wouldn't worry about that. Can you see the light?

Not yet, but I feel very contented and peaceful, and yes, there is a spot of light.

33

<u>Lilian:</u> Yes, that will get bigger, and then you'll begin to see someone waiting for you—maybe two or three people, and they can explain a whole lot better than me.

And they'll hear me, will they?

<u>Lilian:</u> Oh yes! Or you'll know what they're thinking and they'll know what you're thinking.

Do you know, if this is DYING, it's WONDERFUL!

<u>Lilian:</u> Well, that's nice to know!

It is—it's wonderful! And I can see them now.
Would you like to come with me?

<u>Lilian:</u> It's not quite my time to come. *(I see.)* I'm someone that can help and understand things a little.

I have to go, because I'm beginning to feel emotional.

<u>Lilian:</u> Well, I know you'll be happy.

I want to look back and yet I want to go.

<u>Lilian:</u> Well, you can go forward first, and then you can look back in your own time.

How Wonderful! How very wonderful!

The Love-connection with her *beau*, as with all *Love-bonds* remained, so he was *there* to meet her and their *Love* can now *blossom!*

This next rescue *(2015/02/02)* is a little different in that the *transition* takes place via a *door,* rather than the usual *Tunnel of Light:*

Very misty, isn't it?

Lilian: You can see mist—are you outside?

Yes—very misty.

Lilian: Can you see your way at all?

I can see a house.

Lilian: What else can you see?

Street light.

Lilian: Is it where you live nearby?

I rather think I'm lost. I'm looking for Michael, my husband. He should've been back by now.

Lilian: You went out to look for him?

Yes, I'm still looking for him. Oh, he makes me so cross sometimes.

Lilian: They can, can't they? I'm going to explain where you are—it may be a bit of a shock—I apologise for that, but I think you've passed into Spirit and that's why you don't know where you are.

No, no, no of course I haven't—I'm looking for my love.

Lilian: I think you'll find Michael—you'll find him.

He'd better hurry up, because I intend to go home.

Lilian: Well, first of all, I'd like you to think about what I've said.

(Jan with clairvoyance, interjected that Michael was waiting for her in the house.)

Lilian: Did you hear that? He's waiting for you.

Well, I shall give him what for—keeping me waiting and worrying.

Lilian: You'll see bright lights all around—very bright lights. *(Jan suggested she should open the door.)*

Who ARE you?

Jan: I'm just somebody hoping to help you, because you were lost.

Do you usually help people?

Jan: If I can—I dare say you do too.

I'm getting really irritated by the second.

(Jan reiterated that she should open the door.)

Sara: Will you do that, open the door?

Who said that? You didn't.

Lilian: Somebody else is trying to help as well.

Jan: It's a big brown door.

Sara: Can you see the door?

I can see the house.

Sara: Go towards the house.

There's too many people telling me what to do!

Lilian: Okay, okay. Just open the door into the house.

Do you want me to trespass? (Yes.) ***Do you really think that I should open someone's door?***

Lilian: If you look at the door now—it's nice and bright. *(yes)* Well, that's a strange door. And that's the door you must open.

Why, what's he doing in there?

Lilian: Well, open the door—then you'll see Michael in a bright light. Remember I told you that you'd passed into Spirit—and you both are in Spirit. You can find Michael and go together.

Well, I never! He is there, isn't he! Very handsome! Well, I never! I must be dreaming surely!

<u>Lilian</u>: No, you're not dreaming. It's where we all go when we die, only you hadn't thought about it.

He's very young and I'm very young—I'm not old enough to die!

<u>Lilian</u>: Well, I'm telling you that you're dead, but in a way, we can't die—we just pass into Spirit and start a new life.

—Full of sparkling light!

<u>Lilian</u>: Yeah, it's a beautiful place.

I can see it's beautiful—I'm just not convinced.

<u>Lilian</u>: You probably thought of it as Heaven—well, that's a very good word for it.

Oh look! How beautiful is that!

<u>Lilian</u>: So, you're quite happy to go and find out more about it and see more beauty?

I do want to go, but I'm still going to tell him off.

<u>Jan</u>: He's smiling and he's saying he wouldn't expect anything else from you. *(Chuckles)*

It's that voice again! Where's it coming from?

<u>Lilian</u>: It's just another one trying to help.

I like you—you're very kind. How can I let you know if I really am dead? (Chuckles)

<u>Lilian</u>: It's just something I know—it happens to us all, as you know.

Well, I know now...

<u>Lilian</u>: I just helped —I'll say I helped you through the door, into Spirit.

Yes, I am going now and yes, he is smiling at me. How can I be cross?

<u>Lilian</u>: Well, he can explain much more than I did.

Can I know your name? (Lilian.) *Thank you Lilian, I'm beginning to believe you.*

<u>Lilian:</u> You're welcome. Glad to have helped.

The next gentleman *(2021/11/15) was aware* that he had *'died'*, but was *not* willing to enter the *Tunnel of Light*, until his brother was with him:

Who might you be?

<u>Paul:</u> My name's Paul.

Paul—I'm actually looking for my brother.

<u>Paul:</u> Okay, when did you last see him?

Some time ago, some time ago. Anyway, are you in charge?

<u>Paul:</u> Well, not exactly, but I'm usually the one that helps talk to people when they come through.

Are you the one who wears a blue uniform?

<u>Paul:</u> I don't wear a uniform, no.

Well, you'll be of no use to me then.

<u>Paul:</u> Can I just ask, where do you think you are at the moment?

I'm at the station.

<u>Paul:</u> Right, that explains it—were you feeling a bit unwell recently?

I didn't come here to be questioned—I'm looking for my brother.

<u>Paul:</u> We'll get to your brother—we can definitely help you, but the reason I asked about the illness is

this is like a '*halfway place*'—something has caused you to die—there is no real death, we carry on and we do go to a place a bit like Heaven. Something must have caused you to die...

I know what caused that! (You know?) *Yes, why are you telling me?*

Paul: You already know then? *(Yes)* I see, so have you already gone over to Spirit?

You mean the tunnel? (Yes) *I'm not going into the tunnel till I've found my brother. I was told I could meet him at the tunnel, but not to go into the tunnel until I'd found him.*

Paul: Well, if your brother has already passed to Spirit—I think he has, has he?

He has, but he's lost.

Paul: I see, so you don't know for sure if he's crossed over yet?

I've been told he's not crossed over, not completely.

Paul: Have you looked into the tunnel? You don't have to go *in* it, but simply look *at* it, because if he *has crossed*, he may well appear in the tunnel already.

I was told to look for the blue uniform, not to go into the tunnel and wait for him till he appears. Once he appears, I can guide him into the tunnel.

Paul: I see, so what's your brother's name? *(Jim)* So, maybe if we all think of Jim...

No, he won't come with anyone except me.

Paul: Yes, but I'm wondering if he knows that you're here waiting. Maybe we can send a message to Jim, with our thoughts—thoughts of *Love,* to draw him close to us now.

Yes, that may be a good idea.

Paul: So, if we all focus—send our *Love* out to *Jim* and try and draw him in. Lots of people do get a bit lost on this journey.

You wouldn't believe how many. THERE HE IS! I can see him!

Paul: Ah, lovely, good—can you *grab him?*

I've got his arm, I've got his arm! Please show me the tunnel.

Paul: The tunnel will just *appear*, just look towards the light and it will *be there.*

Yeah, I've got it—thank you sir, thank you very much.

Paul: Thank you, enjoy your new life—good luck to you both.

Thank you sir, thank you so much.

When reaching out to his brother with his *mind*, Jim appeared in an instant, demonstrating the *Power of Thought*.

Next, *(2018/10/08)* friends who made a pact in a pub:

Paul: Good evening.

Are you talking to me, matey?

Paul: I wondered if you wanted to speak.

I didn't expect this.

Paul: What did you expect?

My old mate Greg—we made a little pact that when I'd 'gone', he would come and meet me. So, where the hell is he?

Paul: So, Greg obviously is already in Spirit, is he?

Yes, we said over a pint (of beer) *that he'd be there when it was my turn. Do you know, I always knew he was a liar!*

Paul: So, where did he get to then? You haven't been able to…

…and I'm not going any further till he meets me.

Paul: Did you pass recently then?

Yes—not sure how long, feels like about a week—I don't know, not long.

Paul: And have you reunited with other friends and family?

No, I'm not going any further, till he gets here.

Paul: Right, it sounds like we need to find Greg then.

(Yes) Have you seen—you haven't been through the *Tunnel of Light* yet, have you?

Well, you know son, that sounds quite familiar, but I don't want to talk to ANYBODY, until he's here.

Paul: Yeah, the only thing it could be—he can come *through* that *Tunnel of Light*—you need to find that Tunnel of Light first, and then you'll find Greg, I think.

I've seen a tunnel and I've heard voices and I'm not going to be bothered with them. HE told me HE'D meet me and I'm here!

Paul: And these voices, you're absolutely sure they're not Greg?

Not Greg. I bet he's at the pub!

Chuckles

Paul: I'm sure he's going to have an explanation and will give you a warm welcome, I just think it's worth another look at that light—if you can see the light and see some faces; you might find, *he's* there, or there'll be someone else, with a message.

Well, I'll tell you what, why don't you come with me and we'll go and get a pint somewhere? Then we'll wait for him somewhere else.

Paul: It's a lovely idea, but it's not quite my time.

What d'you mean?

Paul: I can't go—I'm busy here really…

Everybody's so darn busy! Never got time for anyone else—I don't mean you son, I don't mean to be a misery, but if you say something, you should do it, shouldn't you? (Yes.)

Di: What's your name? *(Who's that?)*

Paul: This is a friend, who's also here to help.

Did she come through the tunnel?

Paul: No, we haven't gone through the tunnel yet.

Di: I just wondered if we said your name, it might help get your friend to come and find you.

My name's Thomas.

Di: Hello Thomas.

Graham: There's lots of us here.

Oh my God! Where have you taken me to son?
Chuckles

Paul: Well, it's okay, everybody is here just to help people like you who need to move on. Obviously, you've died and it's time for you to go…

You know what son, I've just had a terrible idea: What if I've gone 'down', instead of up?

Paul: Well, actually, I can reassure you there. That's a nonsense, a *Catholic church (religion) thing*—it's not like that. *(Oh?)* You'll find, from all the information we've been told, it's actually a lot nicer than anyone could imagine—*REALLY NICE*—even to the point of the *beer*! It really is a wonderful place and there's nothing to fear, nothing to fear! In a way, it's really the *Earth* that is the closest thing to that *'down'* place. You'll be moving *'up'*—I think probably already you must be feeling a bit more relaxed/happier?

I am feeling, yes. To tell you the truth, there's somebody walking towards me, but I can't quite see his face.

Paul: Just keep looking, keep looking…

(Some suggested Greg's holding out a pint of beer.)

Well, I'll be damned! There he is! You old bugger! (Said with great affection!)

Paul: There you go, you just couldn't quite see him at first, but he's there—are you happy to go with him?

Are you sure you won't join us son?

Paul: Not yet, but you go off with Greg and have a beautiful pint or two.

There he is, I can see him now—thank you.

Paul: You'll have a lot of questions and he'll be able to tell you.

I feel REALLY happy!

Paul: Wonderful—so, you go with Greg now then and enjoy that place, enjoy your new life.

Thank you. What's your name son? (Paul.) *Paul—we won't forget you, Paul.*

Paul: One day hopefully, I'll enjoy a pint with you and Greg. *(Yeah)* Goodbye Thomas.

Thus, Thomas and Greg were happily reunited and able to enjoy a beer or two together again and we've been reliably informed that *heavenly brews* are *glorious,* as are the *yoghurt ice-creams!*

Occasionally guides provide useful information prior to *difficult rescues* and on this occasion, *(2011/07/18)* one spoke via Sarah first:

If you are agreeable, we would like to bring one through to you, because this one has been for a very long time in between Spirit and Earth, and we have had problems trying to bring her over to us completely. So, if you would be willing, we would like to bring this one. (Agreed) Could I please advise you that it will not be easy.

Lilian: Right! Did she have no understanding of Spirit?

This one had a most troubled life on Earth planet and she has brought with her all her problems, which she cannot let go of and it is for this reason, the fear that she cannot move forward—so we would be most grateful if you could help us this time. (Agreed)

Rescue begins:

Lilian: Hello—would you like to talk to someone?

My name's Lilian and I hope I can help you in some way. Would you like to tell me your name?

Go away.

Lilian: No, I can't go away—my job is to talk to you. I think you'll be happier if you talk to me.

I said, go away.

Lilian: No—there's a whole group of us sitting here waiting to help you on your way, because you're just wasting time, aren't you? Part of you would like to move on?

George: Lilian is a very kindly lady who would like to help you—please listen to her.

Leave me alone and go away! GO AWAY!

Lilian: But surely you would like to be happier? You don't sound very happy at all. Well, I know that you had a tough life, but you've got to try and put all that behind you and move on. You've got to now move on into the Spirit world, where you can have lots of help, and have a fulfilled life again. It's what happens to all of us. You're not the only one who's had problems. We've helped a lot of people like you, and that pleases us, and hopefully, pleases them too.

Go away, because I'm not listening.

Lilian: Well, I think you are, because you're talking to me, aren't you?

Well, I'm not listening.

Lilian: Don't you think you are just wasting time?

What's it to do with you?

Lilian: Quite a lot actually—we just want to see you happy.

George: We're all part of a very big family, and there's a wonderful life waiting for you in Spirit.

Good for you!

Lilian: A lot of us make mistakes in our lives—big mistakes, smaller mistakes.

Not me—just go away!

Lilian: No, we're not going to go away. What's your name? Can you tell us your name to make it more friendly? *(No.)*

Lilian: Well, that's a shame. There are a lot of lovely people on the other side of life, waiting to help you. Can't you feel the love and the warmth around you? *(No.)* I'm sure you can—there's a little chink there somewhere wanting to do that. *(No.)* Yes, there is.

George: If you look ahead, there's a white light.

No, no, no, no!

Lilian: Can you tell us why you keep saying 'no'? Surely you don't want people to keep *trying* to help you?

What's it to do with you, anyway? What's it to do with you? It's none of your business!

Lilian: It pleases us if we can help you. Surely, it's nicer to help somebody than just walk by?

George: It pleases us if we know that you're happy and I think if you look ahead to the *light,* the wonderful light, you'll begin to feel what it's all about.

I've heard all this before.

Lilian: I thought you might have! *(Said with a chuckle)* Well just please us and listen.

Why should I please you? I don't know you or you—leave me alone!

Lilian: We don't know *you*, but we just like to help people as they go along. Surely you must have had

46

that feeling yourself? *(No)* You liked animals, didn't you?

How do you know that? How do you know that?

<u>Lilian:</u> Well, that's a surprise, isn't it? But *you liked* to help the *animals*, and you really had no time for anyone who didn't help them or be nice to them, and we're doing the same sort of thing.

What are you saying I'm an animal?

<u>Lilian:</u> Oh no, no, no—of course not. *(Chuckle)* But if you listened to me, you could go on into the Spirit world, and *still help animals.*

<u>George:</u> And we have a love of animals as well.

Somehow, I don't believe you—I don't believe you.

<u>Lilian:</u> We do! And there are a lot of animals that come over, missing their owners, and they look for someone to love them.

What are you saying?

<u>George:</u> If you had a bond with an animal, then that animal can be with you in Spirit.

<u>Lilian:</u> In fact, you may find that that's what's waiting for you, some of the pets and animals that you were friendly with and helped.

They never hurt me.

<u>Lilian:</u> No, they don't, do they? I think you'll find quite a bunch of them waiting; and then your job could be to help the ones back on this planet that *are* cruelly treated and when you get there, it will be explained to you how you could do that. At the moment, I just don't know how that works, because I'm still on the Earth.

Well, how can you know? How can you know then?

Lilian: Intuition?

Intuition! Balderdash!

Gary: Somebody broke your heart, didn't they?

Yes! How do you know?

Gary: I do!

How do you know that—I didn't tell anyone.

Lilian: It's just the thought, it's put into our minds.

Gary: You have to heal that broken heart. The heart that is broken can always be healed again—you have to believe that.

Why should I have to believe it?

Gary: Why do you wish to stay in a state of brokenness? Is that really what you want?

But it's my business, and nobody else's.

Lilian: It is, but I still think you're wasting your time, when you could do so much good.

You lot know too much.

Lilian: Well, there! So could you, you see? You would get to know more than we know. *(How?)* Because in Spirit, they will show you. You will become much more knowledgeable.

George: You can make a lot of animals happy as well, if that is your wish.

I love the animals. (Good) *Don't like people.*

Lilian: You must see some animals waiting for you.

George: Did you have one in particular that you had a bond with—a dog, perhaps?

Gary: A horse?

(Much emotion) Yes!

Lilian: A bit of a shock, is it? Part of you doesn't want to know, but I think we're on the right road, don't you?

Sarah: If you look into that light, I think you might see that lovely horse. Have a look, just see if you can see. Can you see anything?

(Weeping) **I do feel lighter.** (Good!) **There's something there. I can't quite see.**

Lilian: You *will!* What do you see waiting? *(Huge sobs)* What do you see? Who's waiting? *(More weeping)*

George: It's a time of emotion, but that's good.

Sarah: If you start moving towards that light now…

Gary: Just let it draw you up—don't resist it. *(Sighs.)*

"The Love-bond cannot be broken. Many people believe the animals do not have a Soul—that is entirely wrong. Those animals upon your Earth-plane, who have united themselves with a physical being, create a Love-bond, an energy that will not be separated. So, rest-assured in the knowledge that you *shall meet again.*"

Salumet 1995/01/16

49

Next, *(2019/03/19)* another strong *Love-bond*, between a horse and a young girl with a stutter:

<u>Paul:</u> Can I help you at all?

Yes, I didn't mean to d-d-d-die. They say there's a li-li-light, but no-no-no light.

<u>Paul:</u> Don't worry, take your time,

Where-where-where is…?

<u>Paul:</u> You want to know where it is. *(Mm)* I'm here to help you and we'll sort you out very shortly. The first thing is *not to worry—y*ou already know you've died and that's a *very good* step. So now, obviously, you've got a wonderful journey ahead of you— whatever you believe, you can now prepare yourself for a *wonderful*…I'm here just in case you had any little worries or fears—nothing to worry about! It's a beautiful place you'll be going to.

I-I-I know-know…where-where-where…

<u>Paul:</u> You just want to know where that light is, where that tunnel is? *(Mm)* Well, for most people, it *does* appear as a light, though sometimes it's even the face of a loved-one, or someone to come to greet you. So, *who* would you like to greet you? Someone that's already passed, who you'd love to see again?

Yes-yes-yes…

<u>Paul:</u> Okay, so maybe even just thinking about that person might help—there could well be a light that appears, but if you've got a good love-connection already, you could think about that.

Li-Li-Li-Lisa—Lisa!

<u>Paul:</u> Ah right, yeah, I don't know for sure who will come, but it *could* be Lisa.

Lisa a Hor-hor-hor-horse-horse.

50

(At this point Eileen suggested Paul put his hand on Sabine's back, to help with the speech)

Paul: So, Lisa maybe…What do you *see* in front of you or around you at the moment.

It's all green.

Paul: And do you sense anyone around?

Li-Lisa.

Paul: You can feel her presence, can you? *(Mm)* Maybe you'll begin to see a light soon, or maybe Lisa's face coming through?

Can-can-can you help me jump on Lisa?

Paul: Well, I'm sure you can have a good jump on her—the first step is to go with her to start with.

My arms don't work—I can't go on her back.

Paul: You'll find your arms *WILL* work now—they'll work perfectly fine *now*.

Lisa's coming down.

Paul: She'll help you, she'll help you and she can help you to learn, if you need to learn again, how to use your arms—they *will* begin to work. Maybe Lisa can help get you up, so you can…

Lisa's a good-good-good hor-horse.

Paul: Good horse—right. So, I'm sure you'd like to get up onto Lisa's back *(Yeah)* and then Lisa will take you through the light. *(Yes.)* Yeah, so, *let's do* that now then. Is Lisa close enough now?

Mm, she's bent down.

Paul: Right, so can you find yourself moving towards her now, moving onto her back? *(Yes)* Right, and *up* she gets then.

Thank, thank you.

51

Paul: And what a *wonderful way* for you to cross into the world of *Spirit, riding on Lisa's back.* So, are you happy to go with Lisa now?

Yeah, yes.

Paul: She's a beautiful horse!

And Lisa carried her *HOME!*

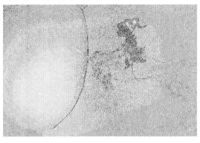

Next, *(2013/11/04)* another *Love-bond* between animal and human. Eileen became aware of a *sheepdog* called *'Bob'.* Then one spoke, asking for Mrs Grimshaw:

Lilian: No, not Mrs Grimshaw—my name's Lilian— she used to help you?

I want her to feed Bob—feed my Bob.

Lilian: Ah! Bob belongs to you!

Yes.

Lilian explained we had been discussing what kind of dog he was

It's a sheepdog—you can see it, I can't.

Lilian: You're the one that can see him now.

No, I can't see anything my dear.

Lilian: I guessed that—you can't see at all. But you *can,* because you've died, and your eyes and everything else will be fine.

No, my dear, I can't see you—I can't see you my dear.

Lilian: You think, because you were blind.

Yes.

Lilian: What do you last remember? Waiting for Mrs Grimshaw?

Yes—waiting so she could feed my dog—he's hungry.

Lilian: Well, I think I'm going to talk to you first, before we see about Bob.

No, I don't want to, you must feed my Bob—Feed him!

Lilian: You put your hand forward, you can actually feel Bob sitting there in front of you.

Yes, he's hungry.

Lilian: Yeah, okay, we'll give him something to eat.

Where's Mrs Grimshaw today?

Lilian: I don't know where Mrs Grimshaw is, perhaps she's a bit late.

Who let you in?

Lilian: If you just listen for a minute.

No, you just listen for a minute—this is MY house.

Lilian: Something has caused you to die. Now, you're going to be surprised, aren't you?

I'm not going anywhere without my dog.

Lilian: No, your dog's waiting, because you know your dog's here. He is waiting for you to *see* him, perhaps for the first time. Was he a guide dog to you?

No—I didn't want one of those, I'm not getting rid of my Bob. He's a GOOD DOG.

<u>Lilian:</u> He sounds lovely. Well, he's sat right in front of you. Do you understand—did you ever think what happens to you when you die?

Of course I did.

<u>Lilian:</u> What did you think?

You're gone and you're gone, aren't you.

<u>Lilian:</u> Well, you start a new life.

No, I don't believe all that.

<u>Lilian:</u> I'm afraid it's right.

How do you know?

<u>Lilian:</u> Trust me, I know.

Are you some kind of magician?

<u>Lilian:</u> After you died, Bob eventually died too and *he* knows where he belongs, but he's been waiting for you. So, he goes to Spirit as well. It's a lot to take in, isn't it? *(Yes…)* But you feel fine?

I feel quite chipper!

<u>Lilian:</u> And also, you can *see.*

No, I can't see.

<u>Lilian:</u> You can! And ahead of you now, you can see Bob waiting for you.

If that was my Bob, he'd be barking by now.

<u>Lilian:</u> Well, say hello to him and tell him to bark. He's probably trying to smile at you—wishing you'd come along—because you and him can be together. *(Now the lady was able see, just managing to speak through the tears.)*

It's the first time I've ever seen him!

<u>Lilian:</u> You see, when you get to, call it 'Heaven', that'll probably make more sense to you, you'll find everything, and your body becomes healthy.

Look at him, look at him wagging his tail! He's beautiful—beautiful!

They moved into the *Light* and Eileen needed a *tissue!*

"We all are *energy* from one *Source*, which would indicate that all species, human/plant/animal, derive from that same *energy*. But of course, when we speak of *colour*, which after all, is colour being seen by the physical eye, then we begin to differentiate slightly between each kingdom. Although I wish to stress that all energy derives from the **ONE SOURCE**, because of your evolutionary plan, the animal kingdom is slightly different in their colours. But I say this to you: Those animals who have contact with you humankind, are apt to draw from you that *Love colour*, which is then shown within their own auric fields. So that is why when animals and humans are in close contact with that Love-bond between them, energy interacts and almost becomes as one. I'm sure all of you have heard many times peoples say, '*I Love my animals more than humans*'. That is because the energies, the Love between each—although in a different evolutionary phase, it is so

strong that the colours begin to show themselves
as *ONE*."

Salumet 1997/01/27

To wrap up the chapter, the next rescue *(2019/06/17)*
was assisted by an *'imaginary friend'* from
childhood:

I don't want to speak.

Paul: You don't want to speak?

I have nothing to say on the matter.

Paul: Well, you've come here for a reason obviously.

We've already talked about it.

Paul: It sounds like you've talked to *others,* but you
haven't talked *here*—this is a bit different, where you
are now. Do you realise what's happened to you?

*I realise that I'm sitting here and I don't want to get
out of this place.*

Paul: Have you been ill recently, may I ask? *(No)* So,
normally when you come *here,* it's because—did you
have any belief about life after death?

There's none what-so-ever!

Paul: Right, you've always believed that I guess
strongly, but when it comes to it, none of us ever
know until it actually *happens*. This is what has
happened to you *now* and you are beginning to
experience… The fact is, your body no longer lives,
but the Spirit inside continues. But, you're a little bit
stuck—we need to help you move on.

I am NOT stuck, I'm happy where I am!

Paul: Well, perhaps it seems reasonable to you to stay
where you are, but if we can show you that there
really is somewhere, where you really will be a lot

happier still. Is there anyone that has already passed away that you would like to see again?

I would love to see my partner Claudio, but I will NOT, that would be a silly thing to say.

Jan: This is also going to seem or sound very silly, but did any of you work with primates?

How do you know I had one as a child?

Jan: I know, because for the last few minutes, I've been seeing the face of a primate and I think this primate has been shown to me so that they can show YOU, because they passed away a long time ago, didn't they?

He was my friend!

Jan: I think he's here to meet you and show you that what my friend Paul is telling you, is correct.

Everybody said he was make-believe, but that's not true.

Jan: So, you had a Spirit of a primate who visited you?

He was my friend.

Jan: Ah! This makes sense now. Well, I'm glad to tell you that that *make-believe friend* that they were sure you were making up, they were wrong and you were right! So, when you said to my friend Paul that there was nothing, life after death *doesn't exist*—well, you just contradicted yourself my friend, because you had a *Spirit primate* that followed you and had an affinity with you as a child, and that primate is now waiting for you to pass over to where you both need to go.

Where is he?

Jan: Well, if you just concentrate on him—remember what he looked like, in your mind? *(Mm)* Do you?

(Mm) He's got the most beautiful eyes! *(Mm)* He came to me, first of all as a gorilla, but he's actually a chimp, isn't he—more chimpanzee size? *(Yes)* He's got really kind brown eyes and he's extending a hand out to you.

I can see that now, yeah.

Jan: Yeah? Well, in a minute, I've told this primate to give you the most enormous *TUG*, and you're going to find yourself being pulled through a light. Okay? Can you see the light and hand?

Yes, I can.

Jan: Right, after three: Got his hand tight? *(Yes)* Two—You're going to be pulled through okay, on three. *(Okay)* Bye: THREE—Go!

Afterwards, *Sabine, (the medium)* exclaimed whilst giggling: *"That was BRILLIANT!"*

Chapter 4

Child Rescues

*D*o not grieve, do not grieve for children who go on. I know how your hearts burst when this happens, but you should *rejoice,* because in fact they are returning *HOME.* Too often we see you grieve, if only you could look on the wider views of things, your lives would be much more simple, you would have less problems, you would be able to cope with life's trials.

Salumet 1994/10/17

Thankfully child rescues are often straightforward, in line with Salumet's teachings that children are *closer to Spirit. Younger* minds are generally more accepting, having not been filled with fearful beliefs. As with all rescues, it is important not to get emotionally *tangled up* in the experience, but to stay focussed on the task of getting them *HOME,* where so much Love awaits them.

First, *(2020/03/16)* a 13-year-old boy upset about his bicycle:

Go away, go away!

<u>Paul:</u> Oh, sorry I was just…

No, I don't like you. Go away, go away!!

Paul: I think I'm just here to help you with something.

No, you broke my bike!

Paul: Oh no...

Go away!

Paul: That wasn't me, but anyway. Did you fall? Did you have an accident or something?

No, you broke my bike, YOU broke my bike.

Paul: Well, I don't think it could have been me, but anyway, leave that aside for a minute. Can I just ask you how old you are?

Why?

Paul: I'm just trying to find out what's happened…

I'm 11.

Paul: 11, right, I thought you were quite young, and I think what has happened—did you have an accident?

Mm... I don't know.

Paul: Yeah, mm, I think perhaps something has caused you to have an accident, it's okay though, it's…

It's not okay.

Paul: Are you feeling anywhere hurt in your body? *(No.)* Okay, do you feel okay in yourself—a little bit cold or something?

I want to go home.

Paul: We can help you—It happens to everyone and what happens now is you need to go to a place to get better, and you should see a nice bright light...

It's on my bike—lights.

Paul: Light—that's where you are seeing the light, is it? Good, well, that's very good and if you keep looking at that light, it should get a bit brighter, because it's a special light—It should become a very beautiful light and you'll recognise someone in the light, who will help you; it may be someone from the past.

It's my grandad.

Paul: Right, it's often…

I don't like him either.

Paul: It's often a grandparent, but I bet he's got a lovely smile for you and I'm sure he'll have a few *very* kind words for you today.

I kicked him once and he didn't use nice words.

Paul: Oh well, that's understandable yeah, I'm sure he'll forget about that now, yeah—we've all done things like that occasionally, but he's happy to…

Are you going to mend my bike?

Paul: I think someone is going to get you a *new* bike, you will find…*(Ooh!)* Yeah, there will be a lovely new bike, possibly your grandad will find one for you, but I think he probably wants… are you happy to go with him on this little journey? He'll explain everything to you and help you along…

He won't shout at me, will he?

Paul: Oh no, no, no, definitely not, you can probably see, he's got a lovely smile and he's all warm and he'll look after you and help you find a new bike I think, yeah—a beautiful new bike.

I can see it.

Paul: Oh! What colour is it? *(Red.)* Oh lovely, yeah, I'm sure you'll be keen to try it out. So, there you go, it's all about going forward now, moving forward into this new bike, and a new journey, a new adventure for you!

Mm, thank you sir.

"There are some who seek proof of the life in Spirit. To these we would say, rescue 'episodes' really leave very little doubt—and what would be the point of making up such stories and audio recordings? And anyway, so many of the situations as well as their dramas, lie well beyond the abilities of those who write fiction."

George E Moss

Next, *(2009/08/03)* a young girl racing on bikes with a friend:

Lilian: Did you hear the lady talking?

No! It wasn't my fault. (Tearfully) It was Amy's fault—it wasn't my fault.

Lilian: You've been in trouble, have you? Try not to worry about it and I'll sort it out with you.

I'm not allowed to speak to people I don't know.

Lilian. No, I do understand that.

It was Amy's fault, not mine.

Lilian: What happened—can you tell me what happened?

We were on our bikes and I was winning and she came and our bikes got caught.

<u>Lilian:</u> Yes, I know, I ride a bike, so I understand what you're talking about.

And I fell off, but it wasn't my fault.

<u>Lilian:</u> No well we won't worry about that.

(Tearfully) ***Mummy's going to be really cross, because it's my new bike.***

<u>Lilian:</u> Yes, I know, but I don't think Mummy will be too cross, do you?

It cost a lot of money.

<u>Lilian:</u> Yes, they do cost quite a bit.

But she didn't even get a scratch!

<u>Lilian:</u> On her bicycle or on her legs?

Anywhere.

<u>Lilian:</u> That's a bit unfair, isn't it?

Yes! I don't like her anymore, she's not my friend anymore, is she?

<u>Lilian:</u> No, well maybe not, but I daresay, in time, things will be okay.

She's not having an ice-cream at my house anymore.

<u>Lilian:</u> Have you got any pain anywhere? Have you hurt yourself?

I've got a bump on my head, and it hurts.

<u>Lilian:</u> So, if I put my hand on your head, you'll find the pain will go

That's magic!

<u>Lilian:</u> Yes, you could call it magic.

That IS MAGIC!

<u>Lilian:</u> Have you got any grandparents that you know?

Of course, I know them.

<u>Lilian:</u> How many have you got?

I've got four. I've got my Daddy's Daddy and my Mummy's Mummy.

Lilian: So, you have got two that you know. And the other two, they've died?

I don't know that.

Lilian: Would you like to know them?

(Enthusiastically) YES!

Lilian: Another little bit of magic…

How do you do that?

George: There are many helpers, you've got a nice helper.

Magicians! I've seen magicians!

Lilian: So, let's say that you are going to see your grandmother that you haven't met, just as a nice surprise!

What about Mummy?

Lilian: Well, that's okay, your grandmother will help you there. You'd like to see her, wouldn't you? *(Yes.)* Perhaps your grandfather will be there too.

They're not married.

Lilian: No, but that doesn't matter, they're still your grandparents, they still know your mummy and your daddy. *(Yes)* Good! And now we'll do a little bit of magic: You can see a nice bright light ahead of you.

What is it?

Lilian: Well, that's part of the magic.

You are clever! You are! I like magic.

Lilian: And you can see a nice lady.

Yes! Two ladies.

Lilian: Two ladies! You're clever too!

Who are they?

Lilian: I'm going to ask you to walk towards them and just go on a lovely magic walk with them.

They're smiling at me.

Lilian: Good! Good! You won't recognise your grandmother, because you didn't know her.

I've seen photographs of her.

Lilian: Does she look anything like the photographs? *(No!)* Well, never mind, I daresay these two ladies can maybe find her for you.

That's nice. Oh, they're saying they're going to take me to my grandma.

Lilian: Well! There you are!

They're going to take me and mend my bike!

Lilian: Oh, are they really? Well, that's even more magic!

Yes! That's good! Mummy won't be cross now, will she?

Lilian: No, she won't. So, you're happy to go with those two ladies, especially if they are going to mend your bike?

Yes! And she said I can have a bell! I wanted a bell, but mummy said 'No'.

Lilian: Well, there you are!

You're really magic, aren't you? What's your name?

Lilian: My name is 'Lilian', what's yours?

Lilian? Lilian, the 'Magic Lady' (Amused)

Lilian: What's your name? *(Tricia.)*

Tricia, well you're the one going into the magic world.

Yes! It's exciting!

George: How old are you? *(I'm six.)* That's a nice age!

Lilian: You'll see other children that have been on that magic journey as well.

Will I?

Lilian: And you will be able to swap stories.

WOW! I've got to go—the ladies are telling me, I've got to go now.

Lilian: Well, we'll let you walk off with them.

WHOOPEEEEE! *(Laughter)*

Lilian: So, we'll say 'bye-bye'.

Bye-bye, Lilian, 'The Magic Lady'! *(Amused)* ***I'll see you again!***

Lilian: Yes! We'd love that! Come back and talk to us again.

I might be able to ride my bike.

Lilian: I'm sure you will. I can hear the bell.

Yes, I can—bye-bye, Magic Lady'.

Lilian said afterwards: *"Well, you can't tell a six-year-old she has 'died', can you?"*

It's usually better with children to keep it simple—loved-ones in Spirit world can explain all when they're back *HOME.*

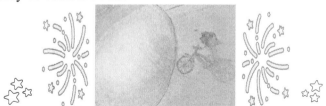

The next rescue *(2019/01/28)* began with *singing:*

Paul: Good evening and welcome to you.

Here we go round the mulberry bush, the mulberry bush, the mulberry bush, here we go round the mulberry bush on a cold and frosty morning.

Paul: That's a nice little song—nursery rhyme.

My head hurts.

Paul: Right, did you fall?

I was singing and I tripped. (Right, yes.) *But I'm very cold.*

Paul: You're quite young I'm guessing? Anyway, it sounds like I'm here to help you to get you fixed up. So, you say you feel very cold and your head hurts. *(Yeah.)* So, let's see if we can help with that—you should begin to feel a real warmth soon.

You won't tell my Mummy, will you?

Paul: Don't worry about your Mummy, she'll understand, lots of children have been through similar things.

But I've torn my dress, she'll be very cross.

Paul: Yeah, but she will understand, children fall over, run too fast and hurt themselves badly sometimes.

And why does my singing sound so funny?

Paul: Well, that will be explained to you, don't worry about that now, see if you can feel that *warmth* coming through, can you feel any of that? Are you beginning to feel a bit warmer?

I think so.

Paul: And how's that head feeling? *(Pause)*

My headache's gone.

Paul: That's really good. Now, if you look around, do you see any little bright light anywhere? *(No.)* Because, I think there's going to be—you might begin to see a light; there could be a lovely lady coming to help you.

I'm not allowed to go with people I don't know.

Paul: No, well that's understandable, but in *this* case, because you got hurt, you *need* someone to help you. If you look, see if you recognise the person. If you look for a light, you might find you recognise them. They'll have a lovely face, I'm sure.

I don't know who it is, but she's very pretty.

Paul: Yeah, she's only there to help you.

She looks like an Angel!

Paul: Well, that's a pretty good sign, isn't it? She'll help you and get you sorted out and she'll explain to you how to get better and everything. So, are you happy to go with her? This Angel?

If she sings.

Paul: I'm sure she'll sing for you. I bet she's got a really pretty voice.

I hope so, I didn't like the last one singing.

Paul: Ah, I think this one will have a really sweet gentle voice. You can probably reach out and take her hand.

I can't see her legs? (Really?) *Why?*

Di: Is she wearing a long dress? *(Yeah.)*

Paul: She's got one of those long flowing dresses.

I feel all right now. Can I go home?

Paul: You'll have to go with the lady—you probably feel fine, but there is a little more healing to do and she'll explain …

Oh, do you want to come as well?

Paul: I'd like to, but I need to stay here a bit longer. Maybe we'll see you again sometime.

Are you ready to go now with the lovely lady?
Yes, I want to go now. (Well done.) *What's your name please?*
Paul: I'm Paul. *(Paul.)* Paul yeah.
Have you got any little girls?
Paul: No, I don't have any, no, I love animals though.
Animals don't sing.
Paul: No, they don't really, you're right.
Anyway, the lady said I've got to go now.
Paul: Yeah, you go with the lady now then.
Thank you, thank you very much.
Eileen said afterwards that she was about 7 and *left happily singing!*

Next, *(2014/05/05)* a young boy unhappy at boarding school:
Lilian: Good evening and welcome. *(Silence)*
Lilian: Do you wonder who's speaking to you?
I'm not talking!
Lilian: Why aren't you talking? I was hoping you'd talk.
I'm not talking. *(Pause)*
Lilian: Are you sure you don't want to tell me something?
No, cos you'll tell them—you'll tell them where I am.
Lilian: I think I can keep a secret—I hope so.

I hate this place!

<u>Lilian:</u> What's wrong with it? Are they not very nice to you?

No, they are horrible to me.

<u>Lilian:</u> Is it a school? *(Yes.)* A boarding school?

(Yes.) I know that can be a bit tough sometimes.

Let me be on my own. I want to be on my own.

<u>Lilian:</u> But eventually you would like to be with other boys and girls, wouldn't you? *(Yes.)* Yes, well if you just talk to me a little bit, then I can help you to be with some other children. They'll be kind to you, and the people will be kind.

Nobody does anything—nobody.

<u>Lilian:</u> Okay, then I'll find somebody that *will*.

I hate this place—I hate it.

<u>Lilian:</u> I want you to think of where you are now, and there's a *light* coming into the room—a lovely *Light—changing colours* sometimes, like a ***rainbow***, surrounding you, and you feel warm and comfortable. You are not frightened anymore. Can you feel it and see it? You'll hear voices calling you—or children's voices? *(I'm scared.)* No don't be scared, because they're all friendly. Coming with the children, there's a lovely lady—*really lovely*. You'll begin to see that lady. I think she's got a *dog* with her too that likes playing with children.

Someone's got my hand.

<u>Lilian:</u> Good. It feels nice and warm and comfortable? *(Yes.)* Good, that's the lady I was talking about. If you go with that lady, she'll take you away from the place where you are—the one you don't like.

70

Where to? Where will she take me?

Lilian: It's to a lovely place where there are other children—it's where children like you who are so unhappy and suddenly somebody realises and comes to take you to a better place.

And there'll be no more horrible kids? No more punching?

Lilian: No, it's far away from there and you'll forget all about it. How old are you? *(10.)* Okay. Can you see the other children too? *(Yes.)* They're nice friendly children—happy. That's how you will be too!

I don't know any of them.

Lilian: No, you soon will. You can tell them your name and they'll begin to tell you theirs. Just forget where you are and go with that lady.

I am, I am, I am …

People sometimes wonder if Souls *suffer* for a long time prior to rescues. Fortunately, this isn't the case. Salumet describes a ***'limbo state'***, similar to the *sleep-state*, where the Soul is *'cocooned'*, until ready—Let's take a ***dive***, and let Salumet explain:

"The problem lies then, when people cannot or will not accept help. They are lost and sometimes we cannot reach them to bring them forward and that is where your *rescue circles* help. But, let me say to you here and now, *no-one* suffers—it is where the word in your teachings comes from, the word of *'LIMBO'.* It is a grey area, if you like, where people come. They neither can come back, nor can they move forward, because their own mind is blocking it. But let me try to explain a little simply for you: You may be in pain, you may have worries, but when you are in your *sleep-state*, does not all the knowledge and the pain disappear from you? Try to imagine a *state of sleep*, where you are *cushioned* from all those troubles, those daily troubles that you suffer from. They are *'buffeted,'* from their pain and their anguish, until such time as they are ready to accept that they need help. I do not mean they are forgotten or neglected—we have Souls in our world, whose *'job,'* if you like, is to help and protect these Souls. They do *not* suffer for years and centuries sometimes, they are *'cocooned'* from all that."

Salumet 1994/11/07

Next, *(2022/07/04)* another familiar theme—a child worried she may not go to *Heaven:*
I will, won't I?
Paul: What will you do?
He's horrible to me, my brother.

Paul: Oh dear, yeah, brothers can sometimes be like that.

He said I wouldn't go to Heaven.

Paul: Well, that *isn't* true—everyone goes to Heaven actually, because that's the only place that we *all* go to—so yes, he wasn't right about that, you *WILL definitely* go to *Heaven*.

Why won't they open the gate?

Paul: Well, sometimes we don't always *see* the gate at first. You're more likely to see a little bright light to start with. It can take a bit of time, but if you look forward, you should see.

He's really nasty, he said they won't let me in, because I'm ugly.

Paul: Oh well, you don't need to listen to him anymore. In fact, you can forget all about that, because where you're going in Heaven, people are like the opposite of that, they're much more easy, lovely people, full of *LOVE.*

He said he would tell on me.

Paul: Well, I'd say you don't need to worry about your brother anymore. *(He's here!)* He's here? You sometimes hold onto memories, but he's not in *this* room, you've been brought to *this* room.

But he's got matches and I'm frightened. He said I'm ugly—I want my mummy.

Paul: Well, you're definitely *not* and he's not really actually here anymore. If you look forward, you'll just see a *beautiful light*, and that's the doorway, the road to Heaven. Can you see a little light yet? *(Mm)* You focus on that, you focus on that, looking forward into that light; you might even see a beautiful lady coming to look after you.

It's my mummy!

Paul: Ah, well there you go! She's a beautiful lady, isn't she?

Mm, she's crying.

Paul: She's pleased to see you. Are you pleased to see her? *(Mm)* So, she'll look after you now, she's got a big hug for you. *(Not George.)* No, he won't be there, so just forget about him now. You go forward into all that Love and Light and your mum will explain all the wonderful things you can do in *Heaven*.

Thank you, I'm going with mummy now.

And she was happily on her way to Heaven/Spirit world/HOME.

"Each loving thought that is sent forth out into the cosmos, is an enrichment, is a growth of Spirit—it is a growth of energy, which becomes stronger and stronger and which in time, will enfold this world of yours. It will be a world of *peace*, it will be a *Heaven on Earth*, as it was intended to be."

Salumet 1997/03/24

The final rescue of this chapter *(2016/09/19)* involves an 11-year-old girl. At this age there are often more questions. Lilian began by placing her hand on the head and gently encouraging the girl to speak:

I'm looking for my sister.

<u>Lilian:</u> And how old is your sister? *(13.)* Right, and you're younger? *(Yes)* Right, we'll see what we can do, shall we? Where were you, when you lost her?

She was smoking in her bedroom.

<u>Lilian:</u> Oh dear, that's a silly thing to do, isn't it? Yes, that's a very silly thing. Do you remember any smoke in the room?

She wouldn't listen to me.

<u>Lilian:</u> No—how old were you? *(11.)* Right, that was a bit naughty, wasn't it? Well, what I need you to do—you'll see a light in front of you with a nice lady waiting there.

No, I can't go, I need to see her.

<u>Lilian:</u> Your sister will be coming too and that lady can help you—you might even see your sister with the lady that I'm talking about.

I won't, because she was all burnt! *(Spoken with tears)*

<u>Lilian:</u> I can assure you now that she's all better.

She was on fire—she was on fire!

<u>Lilian:</u> Yeah, I know, I know, I know—but she's not now, she's perfectly normal, just like you remember before the fire. Now, you have a look for me, look towards the lady who's been helping. Do you see anyone with her? *(A shadow.)* Yeah—the shadow is changing?

Who is that lady, who is that lady?

<u>Lilian:</u> She's a nurse—that's all I can tell you—I don't know her name, but it's her job obviously to help people like you and your sister. *(I'm really scared.)* Yeah, of course you are—I understand that—you don't really have any need to be, especially

once you can see your sister, or maybe the lady can take you to your sister.

I don't understand how she can be okay—how can she be okay, when she got burnt?

Lilian: Well, I can assure you she is—let's say it's a *miracle*—she's had an *Angel* helping her.

She believed in Angels.

Lilian: Well, there you are, so do I! *(I didn't.)* Actually, I think you're probably looking at one now, but don't realise. She's standing in a lovely light, isn't she?

Yes—she's holding her hand out to me.

Lilian: Well, if you'll go with her, I can assure you, she'll help.

I'm a little bit scared.

Lilian: Yeah, of course you are, I understand that— give yourself time—but YOU feel alright?

Yes. What about mum and dad?

Lilian: They'll be fine—you can see them as well, a bit later on.

They'll be so cross—they'll be really, really cross.

Lilian: Of course, they will—I expect you are really. *(Yes)* Still, we all make mistakes, don't we? We do silly things, all of us do.

She was so silly, smoking.

Lilian: Are you happy to go with that lady?

Will you come?

Lilian: I can't come, I have to wait and do another job; my job has been to help you and now I have another job waiting, to help someone else.

I've never heard of this kind of job.

<u>Lilian:</u> Well, there you are, that's your first time—now you know!

Yes, she's right near to me now and I feel quite happy.

<u>Lilian:</u> I bet—and you will be happy, I can assure you.

Please can I have your name?

<u>Lilian:</u> Lilian. Did you tell me your name? *(No)* Your name is? *(Agnes.)* Agnes—so are you happy to go with the lady, and we'll say goodbye Agnes?

If I can come and see you again.

<u>Lilian:</u> Yeah, we can see one another again, if you like.

I'll go with the lady.

<u>Lilian:</u> Yeah, that's a very good idea. So, I'll leave you to go with the lady? *(Yes)* Good.

I wonder if she can help me find my little piglet.

<u>Lilian:</u> Your little piglet?

Yes, a very special little piglet—not a real one.

<u>Lilian:</u> I was just going to say, not a toy? *(Yes)* Well, I'm sure she can.

I had it for my birthday.

<u>Lilian:</u> She's probably got it with her—can you see it? *(No)* No—she's probably got it somewhere safe.

Yes, she said I've got to go, I've got to go now.

<u>Lilian:</u> Well, it's been nice to meet you Agnes, and you'll be fine, and I'll say goodbye. *(Thank you.)* You're welcome.

I'll come and see you again.

<u>Lilian:</u> Yes, please do!

She said I can see anyone I want to—is that right?

<u>Lilian:</u> That's right.

Oh, she's given me piglet! Ohhhh!
Lilian: Is it a pink one?
Yes—my very best friend!

To *wrap up* the chapter, Salumet speaks on the
Wonders of Children:

Children singing in choirs:
"You must remember that most children are closer
to our world, therefore a collection of children that
you have mentioned, would be giving forth light of
Spirit which hitherto is lost to many adults in your
world. Again, it would be a remembering of Spirit.
Do you remember we spoke of the babies who
were distressed because the memory of Spirit was
still so near to them? It is an awakening within
oneself of the childhood of Spirit. That is why the
emotions come to the fore. Of course, it is a
physical act, the feeling of tears, but it comes from
within—the remembering, the vibrational light of
children. The power of small children gathered
together could be used for great things if only they
could be channelled in the correct way, but that is
something which people upon this planet so far are
unaware of, but I can tell you, my dear friends, it is
an avenue that is being travelled."
Salumet 2000/07/31

Millennium children:

"I am sure some of you are aware that since the beginning of this millennium, there has been much spoken about children coming into this world, who are much more spiritual in nature and who in fact have come to this planet to bring much knowledge. This my dear friends I have to tell you is what is happening *now...*"

Salumet 2007/03/12

Giving them Love:

"If only you could look upon these small children, almost like a blank canvass, whereupon the most beautiful picture can be created. That is something you could keep to the forefront of your thinking, because that is what they are, these *beautiful spiritual beings*; and they want only to be loved, nurtured and guided and to know and feel that they are loved. That is all anyone wishes for their lives. I am sure if you were to ask anyone, and I mean *anyone*, even people who dwell within your prisons in the world; what more do they desire than the *Love of someone.* It is most important, my dear friends, that you nurture and cultivate the Love in your lives today, and I wish to leave you with those words, those simple words—and it is a very small word in your vocabulary, but the most powerful."

Salumet 2009/05/18

Chapter 5

Unusual Rescues

Remember that all of mankind has been endowed with freewill, but whatever mankind chooses to do, that is the pathway that each individual has chosen. You know that our world is constantly trying to influence for the better, but we cannot *interfere* in a life—that is for the human being to judge and follow what he feels within his heart, whether you judge it to be right or wrong. So, firstly I would say this to you my dear friend: *Refrain from judgement*, because what you feel to be right or wrong, creates within you a *tension of conflict,* conflict within your own heart. What you must do is to stand to one side and allow these issues—whether you consider them to be grave or not, you must allow each human being their own *TRAIL of CONSCIENCE.*

Salumet 2003/10/13

This is a *colourful chapter*, involving some of the most memorable rescues, like a celebration of the *wonderful diversity* of *Beautiful People* on *Earth!*

This rescue *(2018/10/08)* involved a lady who *'died'* just before performing her *song on the stage*:

Hello dearie, can you tell me what's happened here, what's going on? All the lights are dimmed, everybody's sitting still.

Graham: You can see us?

See us?

Paul: Can you see us in this room, or do you see darkness?

I'm on the stage dearie—the lights have gone all dim and nobody's talking.

Paul: Well, it sounds like, do you mind me asking, were you young, medium or old, would you say?

That's not a question to be asking a lady.

Paul: Ah, it's just that sometimes it helps—I think something's happened to you. Were you feeling unwell at all?

To tell you the truth dearie, not feeling great today—little bit off colour, I think.

Paul: Yeah, I think that's why you've come here, because we're here basically, to help people like you. What has happened—It sounds a bit strange, but it's very natural—people die and I think that's what's happened to you.

I can't be dying on the stage!

Paul: I know! But in a way actually, everybody's got to go sometime and somewhere, and perhaps that's *not* a bad place to go.

But I haven't done my song!

Paul: Right, yeah, I can see that would be a shame. All I can say is, life *does* go on—I don't know if you believe in Heaven or anything, but there *is* another world, where you continue and you *will* be able to continue life and you *will* be able to continue *singing*.

Oh, I believe all that dearie, I know Margaret, down the road.

Paul: Margaret down the road?

Yes, she's one of them 'people'…

Paul: It sounds like you've got the *belief*, which makes it easier, because if you can accept that there is a *beautiful place*, where we all go when our bodies have given up—you move on. You said it's dark, is there a little light somewhere? It may be small at the moment—you may be beginning to feel a warmth around you—you may begin to feel a bit better, even though you said you'd been feeling unwell.

I think it's the old 'ticker-box', (heart) I think it's been playing me up for a few days, but I wasn't going to miss this show.

Paul: Well, it sounds like you've done very well to get to the show at least and yeah, the old ticker-box has got to go at some point.

All very messy, isn't it? I can see it now.

Paul: You can see the light?

No! I can see my bits and pieces on the stage!

Paul: Well, you don't need to worry about those now—that'll all be taken care of by others, and you've got your new journey and your new life to look forward to.

Sara: It's a nice way to go really, doing something that you Love!

Yeah—who's that?

Paul: This is a friend—we're all here just to help to get you *'Home'*, as some people call it—to *Heaven* or *Spirit world*.

Do you mean I've got to go now?

Paul: Well, it *is* your time to go and I suspect that there's a light,

Yeah …

Paul: And there's someone that you'll know waiting for you, to come and greet you and explain everything.

I never thought it would be this easy to be honest with you. I just thought, well, you go and goodness knows what you'll find.

Paul: It's easier for you I think, because you already had the belief—not everyone does.

Di: Was the lady down the road *(Margaret)* a psychic lady or medium?

Maggie? Oh yes, she used to conjure up people. I never quite believed her, but I do now!

Paul: Yes, well you'll understand even more as time goes by.

You sound like a nice young man. Do you like a song and dance?

Paul: Oh, thank you—I do, I love musicals.

Sara: What was your song?

Oh, I can hear somebody calling a name.

Paul: Calling your name?

Alice, come on, Alice, come on.

Paul: That's your name, is it? *(Yes.)* Lovely name—
do you recognise who's singing it?

(Whispered) I think it's my hubby.

All: Ahh!

Well, I hope it isn't one of the others!

(Laughter)

Paul: It'll be someone *special* for *you*.

*No dear, I'm only teasing, it's MY hubby—I've got
to go.*

Paul: You're happy to go with him?

I am!

Sara: Enjoy your singing!

Graham: And your new life!

Paul: There are some beautiful stages where you're
going to, if you wish to continue.

*Well, when you come, we're going to go and have a
sing and a dance.*

Paul: Wonderful! I'll look forward to that!

Put it in your little book!

Paul: I'll remember that Alice, thank you!

*I've got to go—oh dear, I can feel myself speeding
up!*

Farewells (And it's in this little book too!)

Encore Alice !

Thank goodness for *characters* like *'Margaret down-the-road',* keeping the *Light of Truth* shining. There have been many *Emissaries of Truth worldwide*, not just the *conduits for Spirit/Masters of world* religions, but numerous others: *Eastern mystics, Native American and Siberian shaman, African medicine men and women, ancient healers from Sisterhoods and Brotherhoods long forgotten.* In the UK alone, there are heroic platform mediums and many other *trance-mediums*, like *Eileen Roper, Grace Cooke, Maurice Barbanell* and *Helen Duncan* who was good friends with *Winston Churchill*. The trance-medium *Estelle Roberts* used to regularly fill the *Albert Hall*—royalty and politicians were often in attendance. Sadly, most politicians today seem more into *Albert Bourla, Bill Gates* and *money-'masters'* rather than visiting the *Albert Hall gates* to see *real Masters…*

But things ARE changing—Thanks to all Truth keepers and seekers!

The next *(2008/05/19)* involved a character wanting to cross over with his *beer!*

Lilian: Hello.

How do you know I'm here?

Lilian: Well, it's very difficult to explain; you looked towards me, which gave me a little clue.

I looked at everybody. (Did you?) ***Nobody else spoke.***

Lilian: No—we're all very quiet at the moment, but thank you for dropping in.

Who are you—who are you?

Lilian: My name's Lilian. What's your name?
There's George sat next to you, the other side.

George: Hello.

Lilian: The rest are my friends. Can we help you in
any way?

I don't know.

Lilian: You don't know? I think you need a little bit
of help; that's why you've come to talk to us. What
do you last remember?

Talking to you.

Lilian: Nothing before that? Had you been feeling
unwell—hurt yourself in any way? You felt a need to
come and talk to me—do you wonder why you're in
my house?

In your house? It's a Public House. (Pub/bar)

Lilian: Well, you could say that—I've got friends
come in. Did you feel unwell when you were in the
public house—a pain of any sort?

*I remember moaning about the beer—yeah, I did—
moaned about the beer!*

Lilian: Well, I may have got a little bit of a surprise
for you, but something—maybe a heart-attack, has
caused you to die. *(No.)* I know it sounds crazy,
because you're talking to me, I know, but we can't
die really, we leave the physical body behind and
then have a spiritual body. So, you now belong in the
next phase of life, which we call the Spirit world.

No—don't believe all that.

Lilian: That's it, it's where everyone goes, it's
something we all do, automatically. But a lot of
people like you, probably hadn't even thought about

86

it, what would happen if you die and so on, so it's a bit of a surprise—but I can assure you, it's a *nice* surprise.

No…

<u>George:</u> Life continues—just a little different.

No, no, no, no, no, no!

<u>Lilian:</u> It's yes, yes, yes, I'm afraid. *(Chuckle)* Do you know anyone that's died before you, because they may be waiting?

As long as it's not my old man.

<u>Lilian:</u> Okay, *(Chuckle)* anyone else?

Lots of people. (Good.) *Of course, we all die—that's a stupid question!*

<u>Lilian:</u> Yeah, we all do—but *you* did think what happened *when* you die, did you? You just thought, that's a finish—but it's not, you see.

How can I be dead, if I'm talking to you? Don't talk stupid.

<u>Lilian:</u> Yes, it does sound silly, doesn't it?

<u>George:</u> Well, that's it, life continues.

Who's this?

<u>Lilian:</u> That's George. Can you tell me your name please and I may be able to help you a little further.

What good will that do?

<u>Lilian:</u> It'll help me.

Toby.

<u>Lilian:</u> Toby—so okay, what if I said to you, the reason you can talk to me, is because the lady that you're speaking through—now this is a *lady—(No!),* it is—you feel her hair. *(Pause—Toby feels Eileen's/the medium's hair)* You see, she's got lady's

hair. She's got a necklace—can you feel the necklace around her neck?

I ain't no poof!

Lilian: No, you're not, but she's kind enough to let you use her voice just to talk to me. In other words, she's a medium—did you ever hear of mediums?

No, I…

Lilian: Well, that's how you're talking to me.

Get me out of this, get me out of this!

Lilian: That's fine—now someone will be waiting to take you further into the Spirit world. Ahead of you, you can see a light, can't you, a bright light?

Bleedin' light…

At this point another spoke via the medium Sue:

He can see me as well—he can see me.

Who's that?

He can see me but he doesn't want to see me, he's been seeing me for a long time but he won't admit it, will you? Come on, you won't admit you can see me, will you?

(Words muttered quietly—unclear on recording)

Ah you see, full of your foul language when you think you can get away with it.

Lilian: It really is nothing to worry about, it's just starting another life.

Come on, you can see me—been waiting for you.

Jesus!

Yeah, it's me—no good you hiding behind all that bad language. Those days are past my lad, those days are past. Come on, you can see me and you can see the light and you can feel it…

I'm talking to the lady.

<u>Lilian</u>: Yeah, but also listen to your friend.

Friend? What friend?

<u>Lilian</u>: Well, someone you know then—they're trying to help you. Please believe what I'm telling you.

If I go to the light?

<u>Lilian</u>: Yeah, then someone can explain to you a lot better than I can.

Come on my lad, come on!

Can you not get rid of him! (Whispered)

<u>Lilian</u>: *(Chuckle)*

(The one via Sue continues to encourage Toby to come.)

I don't wanna be a woman!

<u>Lilian</u>: No, no, no, you're not, you're not, but she's kind enough to let you use her voice-box, so that you could talk to me, for all the explaining—but no, no, you don't need to worry about things like that.

Do you promise?

<u>Lilian</u>: Yes—you'll be pleasantly surprised. *(You promise?)* Yep, I promise.

I'll hold you responsible.

<u>Lilian</u>: Perhaps you'll be brave enough to come back one day *(I'll do that…)* and explain a little more to us. We wish you luck.

What about my beer? Can I take that?

<u>Lilian</u>: Yep—go and enjoy yourself.

I'm feeling a bit woozy now.

<u>Lilian</u>: Well, we'll say cheerio and maybe you'll call in again one day. *(Poor woman.)* What did you say?

Poor woman! (Referring to the medium Eileen)

Lilian: She won't mind—she's very kind—kind enough to let you use her *voice*—it's the only way that I could *hear*.

George: Yes, it's just that you're being helped by kind ladies.

It's him again! (Chuckles)

Lilian: That's George.

George—alright George, I'm going. (Good)—*I can feel myself going somewhere.*

George: Enjoy the journey.

Oh, there he is again. (Chuckles) Alright, I'm going—I'm coming.

Lilian: Right, we'll say cheerio.

What's your name? (Lilian.) *I'll remember you, Lilian.*

Lilian: Yeah—I'll remember you, Toby. Call in again. *(Mm.)*

Thus merrily did Toby pass proudly into the Light, holding aloft his trusty beer!

Understandably, Toby felt uncomfortable having to speak through Eileen, a *female* medium and it may be of interest to see what Salumet says about *Gender:*

"**Your Spirit is neither male nor female, it is both. So, if you can look upon yourselves in that manner,**

90

your lives would be so much simpler. You would
have the understanding of each other, you would
be *kinder.*

We see so much disagreement between your sexes;
try to *feel,* try to *understand* and see yourself as
someone *without gender,* then you will really
feel that *SPIRIT SELF,* which after all, is the most
important part of *you.*"

Salumet 1995/08/28

This simple truth that we are essentially *genderless
beings*, may help untangle issues around gender—
changing the *BODY* - changing the *MIND*… It's not a
case of *'one or the other'*, we are *ALL* *'both'*. The
physical body is an *instrument* best played in *stereo,*
with a *groovy blend* of *treble* and *bass.* The great
Louis Armstrong blew his *trumpet* with beautiful *Yin*
and *Yang* energy—wherever the *music took* him—
and he *still does in Spirit world!*

What wonderful worldzzz!

This next rescue *(2005/11/07)* involves a *disgruntled
baker* worried about his tarts!
Coughing—Lilian offers a drink of water.
No—there ain't nothing wrong with my pastry!
<u>Lilian:</u> You make nice pastry, do you?
**Just 'cos I've got a cough, no need to say my
pastry's no good. Who do they think they are
anyway? Stuck up toffs!**

Lilian: Who's saying that to you?

What, that my pastry's no good? Ahhhh! I don't want to talk about them.

(Someone else in room coughed)

There's another cough—who did that?

Lilian: It's catching. *(Chuckles)* That's what you were doing, is it, making pastry?

I make the best pastry around.

Lilian: Do you?

Yeah, I do—but now I'm in a lot of trouble, because of this cough—nothing wrong with a cough, is there—a bit of spit and cough—what's wrong with that? Who are you anyway? What are you doing in here?

Lilian: I thought you were going to say that. Well, I think I'm here to help you, if you'll listen to me and I think you will.

No, no—you bugger off!

Chuckle

Lilian: No, I think you'll be wise to listen.

If you think you're getting my pastry for nothing, think again.

Lilian: It would be nice to have some of your apple tarts…

Who said they're apple? Who told you that? Who told you that?

Lilian: I don't know—are they apple? *(Yes)* Nice apple tarts. The cough that you've been having has been getting worse and worse, hasn't it?

Ah! Don't worry about that, don't worry about that—I'm okay—a good cough and a spit in the morning, sets me up, yeah. Don't worry about it.

Lilian: I think your cough got worse and worse and something caused you to die.

What!

Lilian: I thought you'd be surprised.

Died?

Lilian: You've left the physical body and you're now in the Spiritual body. You really hadn't thought much about where you were going to go when you died, did you? You thought that was the finish?

I don't know who you are, but you're talking stuff and nonsense.

Lilian: I'm just a friend, hoping to help you.

After my apple pie, I know!

Chuckles

Lilian: Well, that would be nice…

Nothing wrong with my pastry, nothing at all.

Lilian: But where you belong now is the Spirit world; when we leave the planet Earth…

What's this Spirit—what's this Spirit world?

Lilian: Well, we're made up of two things, the physical and the spiritual; the physical bit of you has just died, but the Spirit moves on and you should be seeing a light in front of you—probably people there that you'll recognise and have already gone into the Spirit world.

Look, you're not bringing any friends. I was just getting round to offering you a tart, but now you're bringing friends, I'm going to say 'no'.

Lilian: You can offer me a tart in a minute, but tell me if you can see a bright light?

Where am I supposed to look?

Lilian: Look ahead of you—you'll feel very comforted by that light.

Yeah, I can see a spark, yeah.

Lilian: It'll get brighter and brighter, until you see figures in the light. They're waiting to help you.

I don't make much of this at all.

Lilian: They'll explain a lot better than I can.

Who are you anyway?

Lilian: Well, my name's Lilian and I haven't died yet, but you've been brought back, just so that I can talk to you and tell you what's happened.

I don't know about this—I'm not convinced about this at all.

Lilian: Have any of your family gone before you?

Of course they've all gone before me!

Lilian: Well, some of those will be waiting for you.

Ahh, some of the buggers, I don't want to see.

Lilian: Some of your apple pies, you'll see.

(Chuckles) Yeah, Henry—Henry I can see—good old boy.

Lilian: Are you beginning to understand? *(What?)* If you can see Henry, Henry went before you, didn't he?

(Chuckle) It's a bit of a shocker, yeah.

Lilian: Think of all the good times ahead of you, catching up on old times.

Do you know what? That cough's gone.

Lilian: Good, you won't be needing that cough any more.

How come, how come it's gone?

Lilian: Well, you won't have a cough when you get into the Spirit world; all the aches and pains are gone.

The only spirits I know is a drop of rum!

<u>Lilian:</u> *(Chuckles)* Well…

And a little bit of brandy in the apple tarts—that's my secret…

<u>Lilian:</u> Is there anybody waiting?

Yeah, he's telling me to go with him.

<u>Lilian:</u> Good, are you happy to do that, are you?

He's not changed one bit—he's calling me a stubborn so and so. Alright, I'll go and see what it's all about. But don't you be touching my pastry!

<u>Lilian:</u> *(Chuckle)* No—anyway, off you go.

You're quite a nice little thing—somebody's telling me, she's a nice little thing. Well, I don't know about that. I'm going now—I'll be watching you.

<u>Lilian:</u> What was your name?

What's it matter to you?

<u>Lilian:</u> So that I can say, goodbye, whatever…

My name's Billy.

<u>Lilian:</u> Right, well, cheerio then Billy and good luck.

Yeah—probably need it—yeah, alright, alright, I'm coming. Always in a hurry, always in a hurry…

This rescue was probably from years ago, so Billy would have been in the '*limbo sleep-state*', mentioned in chapter 4, lovingly *wrapped up* with his pastries, until ripe for rescue.

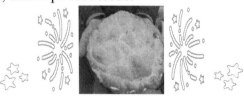

Next, *(2016/10/24)* a boss *obsessed* with his *clock:*

<u>Lilian:</u> Good evening. Thank you for coming.

I'm looking for the clock. What have you done with my clock?

<u>Lilian:</u> Where do you think—do you think you're in your room?

No, I'm not in my room, I'm in the office! And I always have my clock on the wall.

<u>Lilian:</u> Do you know where you are now?

Yes, I do; at my desk in my office—without a clock.

<u>Lilian:</u> Did you feel unwell at one point?

No, but I feel unwell now, because I do not have my clock on the wall! And without the clock, how can I tell if the people are late?

<u>Lilian:</u> Yes, I see what you mean. *(Yes.)* But if we could forget that for a moment...

Well, that is quite difficult to forget, because I have to pay these people and I don't want to pay them for what they haven't done!

<u>Lilian:</u> Yes, I understand—did you ever wonder what would happen if you died? I know it's a strange question at the moment, but bear with me, did you even wonder? *(No.)* Gave it no thought at all?

No. Why should I, because I'm not ready to go just yet anyway.

<u>Lilian:</u> Well, at some point, we all have to go, and the reason you're talking to me is so that I can help you understand that's what's happened to you.

What do you mean 'happened to me'?

<u>Lilian:</u> Well, I think you probably had a heart-attack or something quite suddenly, and that's what's happened to you and you belong now in Heaven; did you ever think of Heaven? *(No.)* Or another place

where you would go when you're pure Spirit? *(No.)* You never thought about it, you probably thought it was rubbish.

I didn't even think about it—just more concerned about where my clock's gone.

Lilian: I know, I know, but I want you to think about it and think of where you are at the moment.

I just told you, I'm sitting at MY desk without MY clock!

Lilian: But if you think carefully, you're *not* in your office anymore, you're in a bright place, feeling quite well.

I can't understand what you're talking about, because I can see my desk and there's no window, so how can I see if it's bright outside? I can only see that there's no clock.

Lilian: Yes, but I'm afraid that's what's happened, so I hope you're going to listen to me sooner rather than later.

Well, let's put it this way: I'll listen to you if you find my clock.

Lilian: We'll find your clock if you want one, but first of all, if I put my hand here it may help you. I want you to look ahead of you for a bright light; never mind where you are, just look for the bright light— may not be very strong at first.

Where the clock was?

Lilian: If you like, and you'll feel a really lovely feeling around you, a great Love, which you never felt before. Can you feel it? A feeling you've never had before? *(That's true.)* Good. Look towards the clock—which will turn into a nice bright light, and

97

somebody in that light will be waiting to explain what you do next; because the top and bottom of it is we cannot die, we just leave the old body behind and take on a new one.

Ah ha! I can see the clock; I can see the clock!
Good.) *Yeah, that lady's got my clock!*
Lilian: I was gonna say, who's with the clock?
That lady's got my clock!
Lilian: And she's smiling at you and saying 'follow me'.
You're right lady, thank you, you've found my clock!
Lilian: I'm pleased you've got your clock, but do you begin to understand, we all finish with the physical life at some time...
I don't know if I quite understand what you're talking about.
Lilian: Maybe this lady can help you understand.
She said I can have my clock back if I go with her.
Lilian: Good idea. I'm glad you got your clock back.
Yeah, so am I.

We discussed later how *daily life* can *revolve* around *clocks* and the *'God of money'*, rather than being in the *present/NOW*.

"I wish to remind all of you, no matter your circumstance, to live in the moment, to live in the *here and now*; and although some of you feel that you already do, let me assure you that you are not

quite there.... *Live* in the *Moment,* and I know
some of you will be saying: *'But how can we—life
is so busy...'* Yes, but you are missing out on *life*
as it *should* be. Every sacred moment counts. You
can achieve whatever you wish and you can have
the health that you desire, but do not rush into
something far ahead, to forgo and leave behind
what you should be learning. That is all that we
wish for you, that you *attempt* to *live* in this
manner."

Salumet 2018/08/13

The next rescue *(2014/04/28)* was unusual, involving
a *Soul fragment*:

Lilian: Good evening. *(Long pause)* Is there anything
you'd like to talk about? *(Further pause)* Do you
wonder where you are and why I'm talking to you?
Are you frightened at all? *(No.)* Good.

(A very whispery voice as if from far away)

I'm watching the picture show—lots of people.

Lilian: When you say, *'watching a lot of people'*—
could you explain a little more? Is it people in the
room with us that we can't see?

**I don't know them—passing quickly. Man in yellow
shirt.**

Lilian: Sorry if we're disturbing you a bit. Do you
know where you've come from?

Not sure—not sure.

Lilian: So, do you think you are still in a physical
body?

No, I'm not physical, but I'm a little lost.

Paul: Where is it you want to be?

I am looking for one in a silver coat.

Lilian: And that silver coat would be one in Spirit?

Yes. Can you help me find them?

Lilian: Someone in a silver coat? *(Yes.)* Do you realise that you are talking to someone physical?

Yes, yes, I do.

Lilian: I would think someone in Spirit, maybe could help you?

YOU help me.

Lilian: Well, we'll do our best. This is a friend of yours?

No—part of me.

Lilian: Oh, a *PART* of you.

Yes—we need to join together.

Lilian: This is something we haven't encountered before, so you'll have to forgive us for being a bit slow here.

Paul: What can you see around you now?

People.

Paul: But not the person you're looking for—

No—I'm travelling—help me, then I can move forward.

Lilian: I see, to move forward you need this other person with you—or to be part of you? *(Yes.)*

Paul: If you focus on *this other person* with your *Thought.*

Lilian: Can you send Love to the other part of you? You know, enclose them with your *Love?*

I'm trying.

Paul: Good, well maybe we can help you—give you a little bit more *energy* to focus on this individual.

Lilian: Perhaps if I put my hands just on the top of your medium's head...

That's better—much clearer. People have stopped now.

Lilian: So, are you together—have you joined up?

Paul: Can you feel them a little bit closer now?

(Yes—yes.) Yeah, I'm sure they're drawing closer to you now.

NOW I feel complete.

Lilian: Well, that's lovely. We'd like to thank you for the help you've given us in another step forward in our thinking.

I knew you would help me—I thank you—all of you.

We asked Salumet about Soul fragments / Soul retrieval:

Serena: The fragment of *Soul* that was rescued, is that the same as the *Soul Retrieval* that shaman talk about?

"Yes, exactly the same, it is as simple as that. It is something that not all people recognise, but it is there and it happens often.

And remember—or perhaps you do not remember—that the Soul has many aspects. Therefore, it is feasible that you can lose an aspect

---

[3] Photo taken in Lhasa – Tibet—thick with incense.

of the Soul. I do not actually like the word 'lose'—
that is not quite correct; it is a disconnection for a
very short time—that is what it is."

Salumet 2014/05/10

Next, *(2017/10/29)* an *upper-class* lady, not used to
being told what to do:

Lilian: Hello, thank you for being here with us.

And who might you be?

Lilian didn't hear this—Sarah repeated it for her

Lilian: I'm sorry, I'm a bit deaf.

I don't need to know that information.

Lilian: No, but it shows you that I don't always hear
what people say—I'll try a little harder.

Well, I certainly didn't ask you to listen, did I?

Lilian: My name's Lilian, if that's any help, can you
tell us your name?

No, I will not!

Lilian: That's not very friendly.

It isn't, is it? I will not be told what to do.

Lilian: Do you know where you are? *(Of course!)*
You do—you know you're sat with us, in a room?

With us? Who's us?

Lilian: Oh, there is a room full of people here.

Well they've got no right to be here!

Lilian: Where do you think you are?

In my chair.

Lilian: Right OK, so did you ever think what would
happen when you die?

Well of course everyone does, don't they?

Lilian: Yeah, what did you think?

Well, not a lot.

Lilian: You thought it was the end?

Of course it's the end! If you've died, it's the end!

Lilian: You didn't think of the spiritual side of you?

No, I don't believe in all that stuff and nonsense.

Lilian: Well, that's what's happened to you, you're sat in this room with us and our job is to help people like you that hadn't even thought about another life when you die—that's what's happened.

(Deep breath) I'm really losing my patience!

Lilian: Well, join the club! Yes, I wish you'd give it a thought, because this is really quite serious and I don't want you to go away and not know where you are.

You're quite a force, aren't you?

Lilian: I try to be—I think you are too.

I think I may even get to like you.

Lilian: Yes, good, but no, seriously there's the physical side of us which you've left…

And no good to anything either!

Lilian: And then, there's a spiritual side, and you now belong in the spiritual side of life—call it Heaven if you like.

You sound like that silly old vicar down the road.

Lilian: Well, no, forget the *vicar*—is there anyone you'd like to see? Someone that's died before you, and I'll bet you, you'll see them waiting—someone you were very fond of?

Well of course, I would wish to see Sir Henry, if I could, but I'm not sure that will happen.

Lilian: I think you will. *(You do?)* Yes, positive, now you're feeling very well—no aches and pains, *(No)* all that's gone. *(That's true.)* And if you look ahead

103

of you, you should see a light—maybe small to begin with, but it's growing.

I do hate to be told off.

Lilian: Well just listen and you'll be pleased at the end.

Ok, I really rather like you.

Lilian: In that light, *(Yes.)* who and what can you see?

Well, it's blue in the centre.

Lilian: Carry on looking.

Yes, yes, it's very bright, I feel like I want to go there.

Lilian: That's right, and you'll probably see someone in a moment—Sir Henry?

Well, I would like you to come with me.

Lilian: Well, I do have a few more jobs to do, like helping people that didn't believe in Spirit, didn't give it a thought, but we all go the same way.

So what's on the other side of the light?

Lilian: Well, I'm hoping you'll see your friend, or your husband or whatever.

My friend? How disgraceful!

Lilian: He was your husband, was he?

He was my husband!

Lilian: Ah right, well I'm hoping he's waiting to help you; he should be there waiting for you.

Well, I can see some movement, and I am, I am keen to go forward I think…

Lilian: Yes, that's good, that's all we need to know is that you're going to go forward. Your earthly life is finished with and, you'll live another life in Spirit. In other words, we can't really die, it's just different—

you're going *Home*—a lot of people call it '*going Home*', where you belong.

Well, I'm happy to be going home.

Lilian: Good, that's the main thing.

Well, I do, I really rather like you, (Good) **so I will go.**

Lilian: Well, thank you for listening and I hope you'll be happy—I know you will.

What is your name? (Lilian.) **Lilian, yes, not a bad name.**

Sara: What about your name?

No matter! I don't like to be spoken to like that. I do not give my name, unless it is to Lilian.

Lilian: Thank you for that, *(Yes.)* but we're happy to see you go, that's the main thing—we've done our job.

Someone said I was rude, how dare they? By the way…

Lilian: We got on very well, didn't we?

Yes, and tell whoever asked that my name is Catherine.

Lilian: Catherine, *(Yes.)* I've got a granddaughter, it's a lovely name.

But I really mustn't stay, I have to make haste, I can see them calling me now. (Lovely.) **It is lovely, yes, goodbye Lilian.**

Next up, *(2006/05/01)* from the *poorer* side of town, a *prostitute:*

Hello darling, who are you?

Lilian: Hello, my name's Lilian, what's your name?

Oh, this dratted weather getting through me bones darling.

Lilian: Yeah, you're cold, aren't you?

Oh, damn it! *(Heavy coughing/breathing)*

Lilian: Now, I'm going to put my hand on your back and your cough will begin to go away.

It's alright me darling, don't worry.

Lilian: That's okay, I'm here to help you.

Yes, but you listen to me, you don't want to be doing this me darling, you get off home, I'll be fine, don't worry.

Lilian: That's very kind of you—it's easing off, *(More coughing)* I'm here to help you.

Look darling, look at the gentlemen, they'll pay a pretty penny for a pair of legs like these. Don't be worrying, go on home darling, get on home, there's a good girl.

Lilian: I want to help you.

I know you can help me by getting out of me way!

Lilian: If you'll listen to me for just a moment…

No, I can't be missing those gentlemen, no I can't I need the money, I need the MONEY darling.

Lilian: Never mind about the gentlemen, you concentrate on my hand on your back. *(Still coughing)* That cough is beginning to go.

Are you a doctor me darling?

Lilian: Yes, and you're feeling warmer. Think about it.

I can't be warm, I've got work to be doing.

Lilian: You think about it, never mind about the work—I'll explain all about that in a moment. You're feeling warmer?

Yes, my chest does feel warmer me darling—it does indeed, it does indeed.

Lilian: Good, you're feeling a lot better. Do you wonder why that's happening?

Because you're kind…

Lilian: We try to be.

Have you got a little—you know—a little DROP?

(Pause—Lilian didn't seem to hear the question.)

Lilian: Did you ever think about Heaven?

Oh, me darling, there's no such place, no such place.

Lilian: Well, there *is*—some people call it Heaven…

Oh, I'm in Hell, I'm already there.

Lilian: No, you're not, you're on your way to Heaven.

No, I can't be going me darling.

Lilian: Why not?

I've got a little one, I've got to send money…

Lilian: Someone's going to take care of your little one.

The dirty, DIRTY so and so, left us without a crust, so I can't be going anywhere, till that child's been fed.

Lilian: Well, someone's taking care of that, so try not to worry about that.

Who? I don't want anybody touching my child.

107

<u>Lilian:</u> Well, a friend of mine is looking after that child.

Oh, you've got such warm hands me darling, (Good) *warmth is seeping into me bones.*

<u>Lilian:</u> And someone's put nice warm hands on your child.

Oh! Well, I nearly said, 'Thank the Lord', but I don't believe in him anymore.

<u>Lilian:</u> Can you tell me what the year is, you're living in?

It's 1942, yes, it's a terrible time, you've got to make a crust while you can, but I hate it, I hate it, I hate what I'm doing, but I've got to do it for the bairn, I've got to do it for the bairn.

<u>Lilian:</u> Now, what I want you to do for me is to look ahead and tell me who you can see.

I can see the gentlemen.

<u>Lilian:</u> You can see a bright light and a gentleman...

No, I can see the gentlemen.

<u>Lilian:</u> Can you see a bright light around him? *(No.)* Is it someone you recognise?

No, I don't know anybody me darling, I don't know anybody.

<u>Lilian:</u> You must know someone. How about your mother?

Oh, she's probably still back in Ireland, the old witch. She used to use the cobber thing, the wooden cob on my back—she was a wicked witch. No, don't want to be seeing her me darling, I'll take you any time.

Chuckles

Lilian: Well, I have a nice friend waiting for you and where you *belong* is in the Spirit world. Something has caused you to die, probably that nasty cough …

No, I can't be dying, I don't have time to be dying.

Lilian: Well, we all have to die, we all have our time for it—the cough's gone and you're feeling warmer.

I am, I am indeed I am.

Lilian: That's a miracle, isn't it? Now, how do you suppose that has happened? Somebody from the Spirit world, as we call it, has helped you and they're waiting for you.

Now, now just a bleeding minute, you're confusing me, you're confusing me—hold on, hold on, hold on…

Lilian: Think about what I've said—something has caused you to die.

Well, it's funny, because all the men I've been talking to, me darling, are not answering me back— I thought I'd lost my good looks! What am I going to do? What shall I do? Tell me what should I do?

Lilian: The thing is we *can't* die, we have to move into Spirit world, we go *Home*—that's a nice way to put it.

Oh, what I'd give for a home!

Lilian: Well, there you are then, you can have any home you like.

I can? (Yes) *Any home I like…*

Lilian: You'll meet other people that you'll recognise.

You've made a few bob then me dear…

Lilian: I wish! *(Chuckles)*

Don't do it, it's not the way to be living.

109

Lilian: Are you happy to go with the gentlemen you see, who've got kind faces?

Does he pay well, if he pays well, I'll go…Oh no, oh I see what you're saying, I see what you're saying! What a beautiful, beautiful face.

Lilian: Yeah, what did I tell you—that's where you'll go and live now.

I feel all warm inside, I feel like I'm glowing inside.

Lilian: Are you happy to go?

Well, just for a minute, don't go. Put that lovely warm hand on my back—oh you're such a darling, such a darling. What's your name? (Lilian) *Lilian, I'll always remember you Lilian.*

Lilian: I'll always remember you. What is your name? (Myriam.) Myriam, we've had some nice names…

That was my stage name, my proper name's Ellen.

Lilian: That's nice too.

I've got to go, I want to go, I'm feeling so much better—I'll remember you Lilian.

Lilian: Thank you and we'll remember you.

So finally Ellen realised that Lilian was not interested in the gentlemen, but was there to *guide* her *HOME.*

And to *wrap up* this chapter, a *'hippie rescue'* *(2022/07/04)* involving *magic mushrooms:*

Did you see me flying? It was exhilarating, and I fell down and look at me, ha, ha! I'm not even hurt!

<u>Eve:</u> *Goodness me!*

They said, (if) you're gonna jump, you're gonna fall and you're gonna die—I'm NOT dead! I'm NOT dead.

<u>Di:</u> *What were you flying on, a balloon?*

A balloon? What do you want to fly on a balloon for?

<u>Di:</u> I saw some children with a balloon, I thought it might be you.

<u>Paul:</u> What were you flying?

I just jumped off a cliff!

<u>Mark:</u> Did you take some drugs?

Well, there might have been a few mushrooms around—nothing wrong in that, is there? Really nice!

<u>Eve:</u> You sound like you're still enjoying them.

<u>Paul:</u> Have you given much thought to what happens when you do die?

I'm not dead, look at me!

<u>Paul:</u> Well, you've been brought *here*, so there must be something that's happened, because you're no longer at the cliff, or under the cliff or anything, you're in this room now. If you want, you can feel the chair that you're sitting in. Yeah, but you're quite right, we don't 'die'.

I knew it!

<u>Paul:</u> We can't, that's right, we don't die as such, because we're Spirit really, what inhabits the *(physical)* body is the Spirit, but not everybody

111

understands that or knows that, it's not really taught properly, so it's a bit of a grey area.

I thought I heard you talking somewhere before…

Paul: Maybe you've been listening in to the conversation? Anyway, that's the good news, we don't really die—but the *physical body*…

That's right my friend…

Paul: …*that* can die. Yeah, so, what do you see now?

So, I just hop into another body and yoo-hoo! Starting all over again!

Paul: Well, it's a little bit like that, but you have to actually, the first thing is, you go *Home*, to our *real Home*, first.

I don't want to go back to that house, over there.

Paul: The Earth is not our *real* home, the Home of the Spirit, your Soul, that's our *real Home* and yes, it's true, if you want another life, you can come back, but first you have a little rest time, in between.

Rest time, what do you want to rest for?

Paul: You'll get to meet your guides and all these beings and helpers.

God damn boring people…

Paul: You won't find them boring—they've got *huge* amounts of Love.

And blah, blah?

Paul: Not too much blah blah—maybe a little bit, but…

Di: You'll be in paradise.

Paul: Yes, yeah, it is paradise, it's home beyond any description. Maybe you can already see a little light in front of you.

Yeah, there is a light.

112

<u>Paul:</u> Let that come closer. *(Why?)* You'll see in a minute, just hang on, have a look.

Well, when I look at it, my headache goes.

<u>Paul:</u> That's right, forget about your headaches now, you won't need that, you'll be feeling a warmth and peace and as you continue to look to the light, you may even see someone, it may be a guide, it may be a grandparent or someone who's already gone over.

Now that's quite interesting, because I thought it would be somebody with one of those white/blue sort of things, you know, those white shirt people?

<u>Eve:</u> Like an Angel, you mean?

No, like doctors and all those sorts…but it ain't.

<u>Paul:</u> No, it'll be someone who'll mean something to you.

Ha! That's Roy, that's Roy! Ha! Ha!! you're there! That's so cool, I got to go and see him.

<u>Paul:</u> Yeah, Roy will take care of you now—he'll explain everything—your journey *HOME* begins…

"There are many ways of opening the mind and there are many, as you have mentioned, which use natural products. But this is not to say it is the correct way to open the pathway of the mind. Remember that the mind belongs to Spirit, and sometimes the use of these drugs gives false impressions. Who are they to say that what they say is spiritual? It may seem so to them, but I would not advocate the use of them. And yes, I understand when you speak of overuse in the western world, not only of drugs, but of alcohol and such things. I would not use any of these to open the mind; that should come naturally to you, because as in all medicines—and that is the word I will use, all *medicines*, there are effects which are not beneficial to the body. That would be my only concern. But as we have spoken on many occasions about freewill, then I have to say to you, my dear friends, that whichever road you take, you ultimately are responsible for. So, I can only say if people feel benefit from these things, then that is the pathway that they must take. Do you understand? It is always better—more beautiful, to see the mind open *naturally.*"

Salumet 2015/09/28

Chapter 6

Shocking Deaths

I do not wish this to sound disrespectful—you know that is never my purpose, but this planet is so *young,* this planet is so very young that all Souls who come to inhabit it, come to *LEARN.* That is what you must always remember about this earthly planet.

Salumet 1999/11/01

In death as in *life,* traumatic experiences can hold us back, until with *healing* we are able to move forward. The first rescue involves a team from the **Chernobyl nuclear disaster**. Due to problems with the recording device, there is *no audio* of the actual rescue. However, when Les was retelling the story, describing a *heroic last-chance effort* to prevent the *catastrophe*, another spoke through him. You may notice the *deep-breathing*, which was due to Les only having one lung: (1996/06/10)

"*I say to you my friends, though you did not witness what this one has just spoken of, you can be assured that it all stems from what you and your colleagues do in this Temple of Love.*

(The 'Temple of Love' refers to a spare bedroom, which was set aside for meditation/spiritual work.)

It was a tremendous experience for the lady concerned. We cannot express sufficiently our gratitude or admiration for her taking on such a task. We know it left her somewhat depleted, but that was taken care of and what I wish to tell you is that the group, whose representative came here and was dealt with as usual, are now well on their way to accepting the new conditions in which they find themselves. I thought that it was only fair that I should come to tell you this, to confirm once again that you cannot possibly ever know, whilst you are in this physical plane, the tremendous work that you all do to help those just to cross the border. We can only ask that you continue to give your time, your energy and your Love in these matters. For this we thank you in advance, for all that still remains to be done.

<u>George:</u> We thank you—God bless you.

We ask God's blessing upon you all. Never fear that you will be left with any definite reaction after such a 'rescue'—all will be resolved. God be with you all my friends."

We are so very grateful to *Leslie, (above)* who began the *Salumet Circle* and was *truly inspirational.*

The next rescue *(2006/12/11)* involved a shooting on a bridge:

Lilian: Hello.

Shoosh! They'll hear! (Whispered)

Lilian: Why do you want me to shoosh?

Shoosh! They'll hear us, they'll hear us—they're coming.

Who are you?

Lilian: Hello.

Shoosh! Don't make a noise! They'll find us! He's looking this way!

Lilian: Who's looking this way?

The soldier!

Lilian: I think you'll find he's gone.

No, shoo—shoosh—don't make a noise.

Lilian: He's gone—gone completely, you're just talking to me.

Shoosh! Shoosh! Look, he's coming across!

Lilian: You're only talking to me.

I know! Don't talk, don't talk, he'll find us—don't talk!

Lilian: There's nobody there—that person's gone.

No! He's here!

Lilian: You can talk to me quite alright now.

No, no! Shoo—please—shoosh!

Lilian: You think about it—there's no need to be worried about that person. He's completely gone—I told them to go away.

They won't—he's just shot that woman—he's shot that woman! Please don't talk!

Lilian: That's alright, that's all finished with.

He's gonna kill us!

117

Lilian: I want you to try and forget that picture now.

I can't.

Lilian: I know, it's very difficult, isn't it?

He's coming, he's gonna kill us, he'll kill us, he'll kill us!

Lilian: It's alright.

He's coming!

Lilian: I'm here to try and help you.

You can't—how can you help?

Lilian: I can help you.*(*

How?!

Lilian: What I'd like you to do is imagine you're surrounded by a beautiful light.

I can't, I can't!

Lilian: You will, you will eventually—I'll help you put a light all the way around you, to protect you.

He's coming, he's coming—quick!

Lilian: No, no, no, he's gone, believe me—he's gone! You can feel my hand on you, can't you? *(Pause)* And you're beginning to feel less frightened and more peaceful.

He shot me, didn't he? He's killed me…

Lilian: You're not dead, are you, because you're talking to me. You're beginning to think, how does that happen? Well, when we 'die' we go to the Spirit world, where no harm can come to you anymore.

Why am I here? Why am I still here, under this bridge? Why am I still here?

Lilian: Well, I'm here to help you and what you have to do is tell me when you can see a light ahead of you--a bright light, and that's the doorway into the Spirit world.

118

I'm afraid, I'm afraid to come out.

Lilian: There's no need to be afraid, I can assure you. Someone will help you to put all this horribleness behind you. The simple fact is: WE CAN'T REALLY DIE, OUR SPIRIT LIVES ON—and that's where you belong, in that beautiful world. You see a light? *(Pause)* You *will.* Maybe a friend of yours or a friend of mine will be waiting to help you.

It's all very dark.

Lilian: No, that should begin to go—the lightness will take over the darkness.

I can see…

Lilian: …see the light?

It's misty, misty.

Lilian: Misty—that's right, that's a start. You'll begin to feel surrounded with a lovely Love—as though you're surrounded by marvellous Love, which you will be!

I can see a tunnel—there's a tunnel. (Spoken softly - Lilian doesn't hear it completely)

Lilian: Would you be happy to go with that person?

Will you come with me?

Lilian: I can't come with you, but a friend of mine will be there—it's just to help you through the door into Spirit world.

You're not tricking me, are you? You mean it, don't you—I feel very calm.

Lilian: You'll be helped all the way, to a marvellous new life.

I can see the light, I can see some light, yes—yes, I want to go, I want to go, I do want to go—please let me.

119

Lilian: Feeling happier? *(Yes.)* Good.

Much—calm, I feel very light, almost like floaty—very floaty—I want to go.

Lilian: I'll let you go—find peace and happiness.

Next, *(2019/09/09)* a traumatic drowning at sea:

It's cold, it's so cold.

Paul: It's cold? Ah, it should be warming up now—you've come to a place where we can sort you out—It should begin to feel warmer.

The sea is so cold.

Paul: Ah, yeah—that's your last memory.

Who are you, who are you?

Paul: I'm here to help you.

I can't hold on—I can't hold on.

Paul: You're okay now, actually you're not in the sea now.

I am, I'm bobbing, bobbing—I'm getting weaker.

Paul: Getting weaker—well, if you're able to put your hands on the chair, you're in a chair now, you've been brought into a place where we can look after you. You're actually in the chair—I know you *were* in the sea—luckily that's behind you, that's over—you've been brought into a nice warm room

---

[4] Pai bamboo bridge, northern Thailand

and you should be feeling warmer and we're here to tell you what's happened. So, you ended up in the sea, did you?

I slipped on the rocks.

Paul: Ah, yeah, right and I guess it was a bit of a shock…

Down by the lighthouse.

Paul: By the lighthouse, I understand. Did you have a belief about what happens when you pass on, when you die? *(Not really.)* Well, you're talking to me now and a lot of people don't have a belief in Heaven and it's a surprise when they die—obviously it caused you to die, but you're still *here*—that's right, we do continue—*life* continues and you'll be pleased to know that anyone that you've known who's died, they're *alive* as well, in this place—*call it Heaven.* And I'm here to help you in the right direction so you can see them again. Is there anyone that has passed on, like a parent or a friend?

Lots of them.

Paul: Lots of them. Was there anyone in particular that you'd quite like to see now, to greet you?

I'm so tired.

Paul: Yes, well, you had a long struggle in the water I'm sure, but believe me now, you should be sensing a *warmth* and a new energy that's beginning to give you a bit of strength again—a little more warmth, and you may even see a *speck of light*—that's how it starts—a little light, which will be a wonderful welcoming, bright white light, like a passageway…

I see it, I see it, I do see it.

Paul: And in no time at all, you might recognise a face in the light—these will be people you've known, probably.

Yes, yes, there's Colin, Colin!

Paul: Right, he's obviously come and will be able to explain a lot more than me…

Who are you? Who are you?

Paul: My name's Paul, I'm just here to help you on your way to this new world, this new *life*.

How did you save me?

Paul: Well, someone brought you here.

The water was rough, (yeah) *and I was a strong swimmer.*

Paul: Yeah, it gets the better of—a lot have gone that way. *(So cold.)* But that's behind you now, you've got so much to look forward to—you can go with Colin…

I want to shake your hand. (Shaking hands)

Paul: It's been a pleasure to help you and Colin will take you now and you'll be in very good hands—he'll explain everything.

It's very peaceful now.

Paul: Good—just let that *feeling* take you.

The next *(2022/05/23)* involves a *young man* in a *motorcycle accident:*

Paul: You're very welcome to speak, if you wish.

Who are you?

Paul: I'm just someone in this friendly room here to help.

Don't tell me it's friendly, I shouldn't be here.

<u>Paul:</u> Well, I am just here to help.

*Don't say that to me. I didn't want to come here—
you leave me alone.*

<u>Di:</u> Did someone ask you to come?

*They said, see that place is much nicer. Well, I can
tell you it's not nice, I don't want to be here!*

<u>Paul:</u> We're all told different things, but the truth that
we know is that the place is a wonderful place.

I don't believe you—I don't believe you.

<u>Paul:</u> What would you like the place to be like, if you
could choose it?

*The same as it ever was. I know I'm supposed to be
dead, but I'm not.*

<u>Paul:</u> Well, no-one really truly dies, the physical body
has to die…

*Don't give me all that rubbish, I've heard it all
before, don't give me all that rubbish.*

<u>Paul:</u> You're not in your old physical body anymore,
but you're still talking to me.

Who are you?

<u>Paul:</u> My name's Paul and we try to help people and
explain to them, because it really is a beautiful place.

*I've heard all that before, it wasn't a beautiful place
before. Who are all these people here anyway?*

<u>Paul:</u> They're friends, who want to help as well.

I don't have friends.

<u>Di:</u> We're all happy to be your friend and help you.

<u>Paul:</u> There's always much more Love than people
realise, up there. You can probably feel a warmth and
a peace that you haven't maybe felt for a long time.

I didn't want to die, I didn't want to ... (Very emotional)

<u>Paul:</u> Yeah, we all have to, but the wonderful thing is we don't *really* die and that's what I think they are trying to explain to you and in actual fact, you'll be able to experience being younger again.

I'm only 21, I didn't want to die—It wasn't my fault.

<u>Di:</u> Were you ill? *(No)* Did you have an accident? *(Yes)* Oh dear, that was a nasty shock.

<u>Paul:</u> These things happen—you certainly won't be alone, there are many who die young.

I can't be an angel.

<u>Paul:</u> You can be all kinds of things. This is what they're trying to explain to you, there are wonderful opportunities, things you felt you weren't able to do on Earth, you *WILL* be able to do in Heaven, or whatever you want to call it, because it does go on, *life* goes on—you're still here talking to me.

<u>Sara:</u> And they don't expect us to be *perfect*, they've told us that.

I didn't mean to do it, I didn't mean to do it.

<u>Paul:</u> When mistakes are made, there's always learning, and that's the important thing... If you haven't met your guide yet, your guide will explain what has been learned from all this. It's all really about Love and Learning, so they will show you how you can grow from it and you'll be able to help others. There will be lots of other young people who have had the same things happen and you'll be able to help them eventually.

I want my voice back. (Using Eileen's voice box)

124

Paul: You'll be able to get your voice back and your body and life will continue. It won't be the same, but most people say it's so much better in Heaven. It's nothing like what you learn at school, it really isn't. It's a beautiful place, full of Love and people. Is there anyone in your family who has already died, like a grandparent?

I didn't like my parents.

Di: Did you like your uncle?

Yes, that's the one constant in my life.

Di: I think he might be waiting for you.

Why didn't he come before?

Paul: Maybe you couldn't see him before—have a good look in the light now.

Di: You feel a bit calmer now.

Paul: You might see his face, or someone that loves you.

I can see something with wings. (My goodness!) *A bird or something.*

Paul: As it gets closer, you'll be able to see what it is.

It's a person with wings.

Paul: Like an Angel or something.

I want to go now.

Paul: Oh yeah, you go—that's a wonderful greeting. You go with this one and they'll certainly look after you.

I want to say thank you. (Farewells)

The final rescue of this chapter *(2020/02/03)* involves a mother with fears about leaving her young child:

Eileen shared the name 'Jeremy', wondering who knew a *Jeremy:*

That's the name of my son.

Paul: Your son?

Yes, I don't know what's going to happen to him.

Paul: I'm sure he'll be looked after well.

I didn't want to die, I held on as much as I could, but my body couldn't take it anymore. My husband is not a bad husband you know, but he sometimes has a bit of a heavy hand. So, what's going to happen to Jeremy?

Paul: Well, in these cases, we have to trust. Everything is already known about—I don't know if you already know about *Spirit/God* and *Angels*, but there *REALLY ARE* those that look after young children.

They haven't been helping me much—I've asked them to help me.

Paul: Well, we all have a certain *'time'*, and nobody knows when it is, but there are reasons for it all. When you go to *Spirit realm/Heaven*, it will all be explained—there are always good reasons why some are left behind and others seem to be taken *early*. It's all about spiritual growth and when the time comes, others can step in and help with that and I'm sure your *Jeremy WILL* be looked after.

Well, I want him to live, I don't want him to die just yet, he's so young.

Paul: Yeah, there will be those who will take care of him, even *'unseen ones'*—you'll be able to watch over him as well.

I'm not leaving him.

<u>Paul</u>: Well, when your body's gone, your Spirit does need to move on to the *Spirit realm*, to *Heaven*, but from *there*, you'll be able to *watch over him* and help. You'll be shown how you can come to him in his dreams and there are other ways to help guide him. Everything is for a reason and it will be explained to you, if you're ready to get to that place. And there'll be a lot of healing for *yourself*, because *you* need to *heal up*—and there'll be a few surprises—*good surprises* for you as well, but you need to let go of that body now. Can you see a light? There should be a *Light* around you somewhere now? And there should be some people gathered, or at least one person, ready to welcome you.

There's my little sister.

<u>Paul</u>: Ah, had she already passed?

Yes, she's the same age as Jeremy.

<u>Paul</u>: That's nice, you'll reunite with your sister and she can certainly explain to you how things…

It's so hard, I really want to go and see her, but I just can't leave Jeremy behind.

<u>Paul</u>: Yeah, as I say, you won't really be leaving him when you go with your sister. Your sister will explain it, but it needs to be—you can't really help him anymore from the Earth, from your *physical body*, now that it's gone.

She's wearing the dress I gave her for her birthday. She's dancing—she loves it.

<u>Paul</u>: And I'm sure she's encouraging you to come as well, isn't she?

Yes, she wants me to pick her up.

<u>Paul:</u> Yeah, so are you ready to go with her then?

I will trust your words that Jeremy will be looked after.

<u>Paul:</u> Yeah—and you *will* see him again.

"Each one of you comes here not alone, not to be left to fend for yourselves. How could that be? Each one when the time is right, has helpers, has guidance at hand. It is only when you become aware of it that it can become sufficient help to you. If you do not open the door, you cannot go forward, can you? And that is what in fact you are doing with your meditation. I say to you all, there will be throughout your lives here upon the Earth, many who'll stand close by, many who will come and go. But to each and every one of you, there is someone who remains with you throughout your lives. But although you may not be aware of them, *they* are your inner helpers and guidance. So much could be given to help you all, if only you will open those doors."

Salumet 1994/11/28

All cultures throughout history have described the unseen world of *Angels, Fairies* and so on. *Energy workers, shaman, psychics,* and *seekers* within

128

science and *religion*, have in their own ways described phenomena outside of *normal perception*. It is *there, if* we choose to *seek.*

To wrap things up, Salumet discusses why life can be so hard:

"Still dear friends, each one of you ponders the question, *'Why is life so difficult at times?'* I will return once more if I may and say: *The power of your mind is at fault, nothing else, no one else—* each one of you must accept responsibility for all that occurs in your thinking. If life situations distress you, you must look inward and ask yourself, why does it distress you so. The answer lies within yourself. Forgive, give Love, and your lives will be as you desire. Love and *only Love* can bring about the lifetime which you all deserve. And hear me well my dear friends: You ALL have the ability and you, each one of you are deserving of the best that the Great Creator has to offer you. Remember each one of you is a perfect form of that Creative Force and in having that knowledge, you have the equipment to have the very best of this life upon this planet. Ponder my words this time; each one will review them in a slightly different way, according to their own progress. But each one will find realisation that what is within, is ultimately what you have made it."

Salumet 1998/02/16

129

Chapter 7

War Rescues

Y ou cannot see these *'waves of hatred,'* as they
travel through your space. This is perhaps
another subject we can go into—but wars are
damaging. They can never be good, and even the
peace that follows, is one of false hope. If only you
could see those people who come to our side of
life, those who have suffered because of wars, each
and every one of you would strive, would do your
utmost to be peaceful. Peace, really should be your
heritage whilst upon this Earth and that is what we
too, are striving towards—*Peace for all of
mankind.*

Salumet 1994/11/07

This first rescue *(2014/01/27)* concerns so many
young people conscripted into the carnage of war:
<u>Lilian</u>: Good evening.
(Pause—Lilian asked if we could help.)
I don't think you can. I don't know—
<u>Lilian</u>: You're not very happy.
***I'm certainly lost and don't know where I am. I
know I'm dead.***
<u>Lilian</u>: Ah, fine.

It's what that man was saying about young soldiers. I wanted to tell him—just because you're a soldier doesn't mean you want to be fighting.

Paul: Yes, I'm sure.

I was conscripted and had to do that—and I hated it—HATED it!

Lilian: Yes, I know a lot of people did—army people.

And I can't move on, I just keep thinking about it all the time—the death, the destruction—the waste of life.

Lilian: What war were you involved in?

They're all the same to me now, I think it was the first one—first big one. (WW1)

Lilian: Yes, it's just that on the Earth now, it's being remembered.

Yes, I hated it with a passion.

George: Yes, we can well understand your feeling.

You see, it wasn't only the fear of being killed by your opponent—it's the fear of your OWN killing you, if you spoke out. It's a terrible fear to live with. I can't forget it; it's like a film that's got stuck.

Lilian: Do you think it's time to move on? Do you feel you would like to move on?

I want to, but haven't been able to.

Lilian: I'm sure you will be able to.

I've listened to people telling me that, but I just can't; the memories are too vivid. What can I do?

Lilian: Well, it's a case of almost forgiving yourself for something that you didn't really want to be caught up in, isn't it?

George: We have to forgive the past, that's part of growing.

131

How do you do that?

<u>Lilian:</u> Have you thought of talking to someone—
another soldier who was on the other side to you, who
I bet feels the same?

<u>George:</u> How old were you?

19

<u>Lilian:</u> A little bit resentful as well?

Yes.

<u>George:</u> Well at 19 you've barely had a chance to
work out spiritual values—one is told to do things by
elders, by politicians or whoever and this has been a
tragedy of our earthly ways, but you can't take on the
responsibility of those who *TELL* young people to go
to war.

<u>Sara:</u> You can't really blame yourself when you were
conscripted, and were living in that age when you
didn't really have a choice.

But I still feel so much hatred.

Jan then began to get clairvoyance: I don't think this
young man blames himself—he can't get rid of the
visions. He can't move on, because he's taken those
visions with him. He can ask to have those visions
removed—they'll wipe that memory temporarily, so
that he can move forward—but he needs to ask...

<u>Lilian:</u> Think of the people you are going to help on
your way. You'll probably feel a lot more people like
you all around, wishing to move on like you do.

I'm not the only one, ***there are hundreds.***

<u>Lilian:</u> Well, if you can move forward and start to
help other people, they'll be doing the same.

<u>George:</u> Do you remember the year date?

Jan: He was in the First World War, but I don't think he actually died then—this is a memory that he holds. *I survived the war.*

Jan: Exactly, but he can't get passed these dreadful scenes in his head. Now, he's come with at least 50 or 60 others tonight, dealing with the same affliction. This is a multiple rescue and they are to be told that they need to ask for help.

George: And Love—can we send them Love?

Jan: Yes—they have to ask collectively and they need to ask Spirit that their memory temporarily be erased with Love, so that they can move on, because where they are at the moment, that help can't reach them. *(Pause)* Okay? You don't need to hang onto these feelings—it's the human emotion and memory that's preventing you from moving forward. So, you need to ask those people from Spirit that you will take the next stage and be helped. Is that okay?

We all want that.

(Jan instructed Lilian to place her hand on Eileen's head)

Lilian: And we do understand. So, if you can do that it will help. *Thank you.*

George: Yes, and we understand and we feel for you all.

Paul: Yes, and you have our Love and absolutely no judgement.

Lilian: And imagine the ones that you can help afterwards—that will be the *healing*. Okay?

Yes.

Lilian: Our Love will go with you and we will remember you in our thoughts, which will hopefully help you along the way.

Thank you.

Lilian: What did you say your name was?

Alistair—my friends call me Ali. You remind me of my mother—Thank you.

Next, *(2013/12/09)* a *German U-boat/submarine* rescue:

I am not sure I should be here—I am not sure.

Lilian: Where have you come from?

I do not remember. I seem to be floating. I can see the water. It is very dark.

Lilian: Did you feel unwell at all?

In what way?

Lilian: In the mind?

Yes. What are you doing here with me?

Lilian: I think and hope that I can help you. You could do with some help, couldn't you?

It is so dark—I do not like it!

Lilian: Why do you think it's dark?

It is because it is—dark.

Lilian: Do you feel unhappy?

No, I feel lost.

<u>Lilian:</u> Well, let's see if we can help find you, or help you to find yourself. Are you puzzled by those words?

I do not know what to think. I don't know. I am lost—I am lost!

<u>Lilian:</u> Yes okay, we all get lost sometimes. I don't know why you're lost, but I'm here to help you and bring you back out into the light. Something has caused you to die. Did you realise that? Had you been ill? *(Jan began to receive clairvoyance at this point.)*

<u>Jan:</u> I've got a feeling of water …

I am in water.

<u>Jan:</u> He is German and he has been in a U-boat. *(I am yah.)* And this gentleman went down with the boat.

<u>Lilian:</u> So, you think you are still fighting in the war—I'm here to tell you, you must have died at sea.

I am afraid.

And there's no need to be afraid—no need at all.

It is cold!

You can feel my warm hand, can't you?

I can, I can!

If I put my hand on your shoulder, you'll feel the warmth going all the way through. Can you feel?

<u>George:</u> I'll place a hand on your other shoulder.

<u>Lilian:</u> Good! Well, while you were in that water, your body didn't last very long—you died at that point. And probably what you hadn't thought of was moving into the Spirit world, becoming a Spirit body instead of a physical one. You've left the physical body behind—now you are pure Spirit and that's where you belong—we live again—the *real* you. You

135

feel warm, and if you look ahead of you, you'll see a bright light.

Also, I can see a body.

<u>Jan:</u> He is not alone! This rescue is a multiple rescue—there's about twenty others, including Russian prisoners of war.

<u>Lilian:</u> So, if we help you, we are going to help the others as well. They will all come with you. What did you think would happen when you died? You didn't think about it, did you really? *(No.)* Well, that's what's happened, and we can help you and the other chaps to move on to a much better life in Spirit. Are you feeling warm and you see the light? And you'll also feel really, really l*oved*—real *terrific Love*. Can you feel that? *(Yes.)* What can you see?

I can see light, I see light.

<u>Lilian:</u> You will see someone waiting—probably several people waiting—to help the others as well

<u>Jan:</u> There's a lady and a gentleman waiting for this gentleman.

<u>Lilian:</u> Parents probably.

<u>Jan:</u> Possibly—they're appearing younger than this gentleman, but I think they're his parents. *(I, I…)* You can see them? There are also several people waiting in uniform, probably people who have served with him. They are asking him to touch their hand so that they can pull him through—it is your comrades, they want you to go with them.

I was scared—scared—scared.

<u>Lilian:</u> That's why you remained in the darkness.

<u>George:</u> No need to be scared.

<u>Lilian:</u> Are you ready to go through?

I feel peace now—peace now.

<u>Lilian:</u> Good! Live again and do whatever you'd like!
(Then an earnest plea) **Help them all!**

<u>Lilian:</u> Yes, they are going with you—they will all come.

<u>Jan:</u> You were the spokesman—they are following—they've all heard what's happened and they'll follow...

<u>Lilian:</u> Perhaps you can have a *grand reunion.*

They're warm?

<u>Lilian:</u> They're all leaving the darkness. They are now *all warm.* You can all go together. Happy with that?

I want to go …

⚓

Of course, God/the Great Creator makes *no distinction between religions, races or nationalities—*

---

[6] *Ernest Moss (Author's grandad) and Navy shipmates—*The *Soviets* lost most in WW2 - *27 million* fighting 80% of *Germans.* Grandad knew well, *without Russian allies, Hitler/fascism would have won.* 20 million Chinese were also killed fighting Japan, similarly *'forgotten' in western 'remembrances'.* Lest we forget--seriously? So let's TRULY embrace it: **Peace and Goodwill to ALL**!*—without prejudice and not just on Christmas cards!*

Russian, Chinese, German, French, African, Indian etc.—all are treated with *Unconditional LOVE, as Divine Sparks from the One Source.* This is being reflected in the *growing understanding* symbolised by the *White Poppy* that *Acts of Remembrance* honour *ALL* casualties of war *equally*, including the *animals!* We are *ALL Brothers and Sisters* and one day this won't just be a *DREAM…*

The next rescue *(2014/02/03)* involved a pilot:

Damned fog—damned, damned fog!

Paul: What do you last remember?

Coming down—the fog—scared.

Paul: And how do you feel now?

Calm—it's still foggy.

(Paul explained that if he looked carefully into the fog, he should see a light and that he had died.)

Who am I talking to?

Paul: Well, I'm someone here to help you—to show you the next stage. Life goes on—not everyone understands this.

George: When we say 'die', it is only the *physical body* that dies—the *Spirit body* continues. I think you are a *Spirit body*, wanting to go forward to your new life in *Spirit*. How does that feel?

Damned fog!

Paul: It should start to lift…

I'm going mad—hearing voices.

George: The voices are *real*. We're here to help you—we are all good friends here.

Paul: It's been a shock, but can you see any *light* around you now?

138

George: Light in the fog?

Where do I look?

Paul: Look in front of you—can you see? There should be a little light beginning to appear now. *(Pause)*

George: It may take a little time. *(Pause)*

Paul: Is it beginning to clear a bit now, the fog? You see that little *white light?*

I've got to make contact.

Paul: Well, if you look to the light, you'll find there should be someone…

George: As that light becomes clearer, you will see someone waiting to welcome you.

There is no damned light. Light? What light?

Paul: It hasn't appeared yet?

I've got to make contact. My name's Joseph…
Where am I? (He gave his full name—edited to respect privacy.)

Paul: Well Joseph, what's happened to you is what happens to a lot of people when planes crash—the *physical body* has died, but obviously you are *still alive*—you *still live on*—it's a stage that has to happen when the body dies.

How can I be dead? I don't believe you—I'm talking to you.

George: Yes, well it's your *Spirit-self* who is talking.

Spirit self? Spirit self? I don't believe that!

George: Well, really there is no death. Our *physical bodies* end, but we are basically *Spirit* and we continue as *Spirit.* But it's that period of *transition* which you are in at the moment, and I expect that's why it seems *foggy.* But if you continue to look

139

ahead, you *will* see a light and there *will* be other beings, perhaps loved ones who are waiting there to welcome you into your new *spiritual life.*

Paul: Someone you will *recognise.*

George: So, is there a very good friend or relative whom you would like to welcome you?

I can see him—I can see my compatriot.

George: Ah! And the light gets bigger and clearer.

Paul: You can see his face now then?

Yes—he is beckoning me.

Paul: Good! Are you happy to go with him now?

I've plenty to say to him.

Paul: Yes, I'm sure you have. He'll be able to explain a lot to you.

Now there's a light! And I feel less fearful.

Paul: That's very good. Well Joseph, if you'd like to go with your friend.

George: When you do, they'll be able to explain better than we can.

I can't feel my legs, and yet I can move.

Paul: Yes, that will be explained to you, that's okay.

George: So, you are going forward now? *(Yes, I am.)* Good, and you're happy with that?

Yeah, almost there.

George: Wonderful! We wish you a happy continuing *life* with your friends.

I'll see you both sometime.

Paul: Sometime, yes—it's not quite our time yet, but we'll be along at some point, yes.

George: We all have this experience.

We'll have a drink.

<u>Paul:</u> That'll be great—lovely. I'm sure there's a good drink waiting...

More than one, I hope!

<u>Paul:</u> Oh yes—as many as you like!

<u>Despite how things sometimes appear, Salumet assures us that there will *NOT be Nuclear Oblivion:*</u>

"Many Masters have come to tread this Earth plane at this particular time. **There will *not* be a nuclear holocaust. That is our mission at this time in your evolution! That will *not* occur.** *But* let me tell you, the Earth is *changing*—and now we get to deep matters again. We spoke earlier of the Earth having an etheric, an *etheric body.* That is the one that will be filled with Love, and change, and that is why we have descended at this time, to bring forth the knowledge to help that *transition."*

Salumet 1994/07/18

(Salumet confirmed this again in 2022.)

---

[7] *Christian Moss—battle of the Somme WW1 (Author's great uncle)*

A question was *also* asked about help from *ET friends,* who we've been told *prefer* to be known as *'Cosmic Brothers':*

<u>Ben:</u> Would they *(Our Cosmic Brothers)* also be here to help us avoid *nuclear war?*

"They would … I have to say, prayers would reach them, but what you have to remember is they are not Spirit, they haven't passed to Spirit. So, they are limited to a degree, although their powers and energy is much more potent than yours."

Salumet 2017/07/31

So, it's up to us *earthlings* to learn to live *peacefully* with all *religions, races and regions.*

It is sometimes said: *'TRUTH is the first casualty of war'*, with *selective information* presented to *'shepherd'* opinions and people *paid to promote* a certain viewpoint, whilst *suppressing* others. A new era of *independent* journalism is evolving, with more *open, unscripted* discussions, so that people can draw *their own* conclusions: *Dr John Campbell, Joe Rogan, Neil Oliver, George and Gayatri Galloway, Natali and Clayton Morris, Tucker Carlson, Russell Brand* and of course, *Julian Assange* and numerous others have highlighted the importance of allowing *free speech* and *open communication.* Nobody has a monopoly on *Truth*, no-one is *perfect*, not even *Mary Poppins. (Practically perfect...)* The best we can do is listen to *all sides*, ignoring all those with *vested interests* and the *truth* will then become *clearer.*

This simple old *Native-American* saying can help with *judgemental thoughts:*

"The finger that points, has 3 pointing back."

If we find ourselves *judging/pointing fingers*, it is *always* about ourselves—a symptom of a *'little war'* burning within. So in *judging* another, we are actually *highlighting* something within that we are *uneasy* about. *Louise Hay*[8] and others have observed that '*dis-ease*', can lead to **disease.** So, when something upsets us, it's an opportunity for *reflection and healing.*

The *bigger picture* of *life* and what we call *death,* can really be a *beautiful journey,* as we move from *fear,* to *loving cooperation, harmony and freedom.* As our *Love* grows, governments will reflect *higher qualities too*! *Imagine* world leaders as *childlike, imperfect beings* like us, *with* their *deeper core part* wanting to be of *service,* without *being able to break through.* We are all *'works in progress'* and as *Jesus brilliantly* expressed it:

John 8:7 NIV

"Let any one of you who is without sin be the first to throw a stone..."

As we *project* purer *Love,* this will mushro*OM* like a world-changing *rescue-beam*, *creating upgraded vibes* and stronger connections. There are *scientific* terms like *'Unified Field'*, *'Quantum Entanglement'*

---

[8] Salumet has suggested the following *positive affirmation*: *I am healthy in Mind, Body and Spirit.*

143

and *spiritual* terms like *'Harmonic Convergence'* and *'Oneness'*—it all points to the same Truth: *All Creation is interconnected energy from the One Source—One LOVE!*

To put this chapter to bed, Salumet speaks on War and Peace:

"Of course, the perfect world should have perfect peace. That is why, when I speak of religion, it has caused more problems than it should have done. Wars are caused by man's inhumanity to his fellow man. They are caused by greed and many other things. There can sometimes be good from these wars, but I would say to you, ultimately, they are bad and not much good comes from them. Perhaps the fellowship of man, together on one side, is an area of good, which results from wars. But of course, that is something that should be taking place in any case. Man, as I have said, has much to answer for. So often we hear the cries of the people, *'Why does GOD allow such things to happen?'* I put it back to you, why does *MAN* allow these things to happen? They have moved away from all that is good and noble. Their lives have become one of greed, of hatred and anger. Too often through your ages, have we seen the results of your wars all over your Earth, not only in your times, but in times gone by, men killing men. What do these actions show? It shows how *poor* in

144

Spirit you have all become. It causes great sadness in our side of life, when we see how much hatred abounds. You were not placed upon this Earth to hurt another human being. But you will say to me, I know, what of these people who wish to steal another's lands? What of those tyrants? They cannot be allowed to roam free.

I say to you once again: *PEOPLE POWER - THOUGHT POWER.* You have within yourselves, the power to change your whole existence upon this Earth. Wars are damaging not only to people, to the countries, to your world as a whole, but the repercussions rebound within the space that surrounds your world."

Salumet 1994/11/07

Chapter 8

Forgiveness – key to Transformation

To forgive oneself there needs to be the awareness and recognition of who and what you are. Without this you cannot learn the discipline of forgiveness. *Forgiveness* is that awareness of *Self,* it is the wisdom of knowledge, it is the seeking of the *spiritual aspect* of oneself. And only when these things come together, will you know *true forgiveness* of the *Self*—only then dear friends, will you begin to understand what it is to forgive another human being, because when you feel the necessity to forgive another, what you see before you is a fault that lies within **YOUR** spiritual being—an aspect of yourself, which you cannot come to terms with. That is why I say, the awareness of **YOUR OWN BEING** is so important.

Salumet 1996/12/09

In the Star Wars epic, *Luke Skywalker* continued to *believe* there was '*good*' in *Darth Vader* in spite of the atrocities he'd committed. Luke was right and Vader actually saved everyone from the '*evil*' emperor, exemplifying the idea that *redemption is **always** possible. Struggles and challenges* are part of the human experience and it is often in the ***darkest hours*** when the *SPIRIT RISES.*

This chapter includes some particularly *difficult rescues*, which readers may find distressing, but much like in *Star Wars,* they *illustrate* the *transformative Power of Love and forgiveness.*

~MAY THE FORCE of LOVE BE WITH YOU~

This first one *(2014/04/28)* was in a very traumatic state:

Lilian: Hello—we're here to help you.

(Desperate sobbing) **Oh my God! What have I done! What have I done! What have I done!**

Lilian: I don't know what you have done, but I think you're ready to get better from this, and that's why you're here talking to us.

She made me do it, she made me…

(Lilian placed her hands on Eileen's shoulders, for comfort)

Lilian: Listen to me: we're here to help you, and you're ready to step forward now and be happy again—to forgive and to forget. *(I can't...)* You will. Sometimes things happen, and they almost seem out of our control…

(More semi-intelligible words and sounds of great distress)

Lilian: Okay, but I think you'll find she's stood there, not far from you, ready to help and forgive, and put it behind you—I'm sure she's somewhere near. You've got to forgive yourself—that's the hardest thing of all. But you can do it, and she'll help you. *(Becoming calmer)* What can you see? We know you are in Spirit as well. What can you see?

A light.

Lilian: Good, that's the first step. That light will get bigger, brighter and you'll be covered with Love. *(Gulps and sighs)*

Lilian: How are you feeling? Calmer? *(Yes.)* It may take a little while, but you'll get there. We all make mistakes. Sometimes they're worse than others, and you've got a bigger one than perhaps some, but there are others with even worse ones. Can you see someone waiting to help you?

A hand…

Lilian: Yeah, take their hand. *(Pause)* What do you feel?

Peace.

Lilian: Good.

A peace. Help me, please help me.

Lilian: Yes, are you ready to take that hand and go forward?

Yes, I'm so sorry, I didn't mean to do it, I'm so, so sorry.

Lilian: Feelings got the better of you. But now you've got to make a new start.

I need help.

Lilian: Yes, you'll get all the help you need—much more than I can give you.

I need to go—I want to go.

Lilian: Yeah, you'll be okay.

Thank you..

When we *'die'* there is no *external judgement*, but we have to *face and forgive ourselves*.

All can be forgiven with *Love* and there are *always opportunities* to *make-amends,* or as some phrase it, *pay off Karmic dept.* We may be guided towards particular work which helps care for those who have been victims. This can happen in *Spirit world* or the *physical Earth*, via *reincarnation,* sometimes returning specifically to help others and learn important lessons.

"I am not happy with the phraseology, *'Karmic debt'.* What is karma, but the result of 'C*ause and Effect*,' something you *all* have. As we have said, you go through many stages of knowledge, of wisdom—you return *many times*, if necessary to learn those lessons which help with the *Soul's growth.* So, in respect of *karmic debts,* I would rather you do not look upon it that way, but rather that you *'return'* to gain more knowledge. To say *karmic debt* rather implies a 'hell' upon your Earth and that is not what your lives are about."

Salumet 1995/07/17

Next, *(2009/06/08)* more *regret* and *self-judgement*—but the ***Light*** is always there to free us from our prisons:

Lilian: Feeling a bit sad?

Aye, and if you want to help me...

Lilian: Well, it's nice to help people. If people are sad, we like to help them.

Sad ... that's what I am ... sad.

Lilian: My name's Lilian, can you tell me your name?

My name ... you wouldn't want to know my name. You wouldn't want anything to do with me.

Lilian: I think I would. There's some good in everybody. We've just got to find it, haven't we?

Not for me. Why would you want to talk to me?

Lilian: That's my job. If people are feeling sad, I try to help them to be happy, and explain to them what's happened to them and so on. Why are you feeling sad?

Paul: We don't judge people here.

Lilian: That's not our job. Our job is just to help and explain things to you.

Sad... sad doesn't even begin to tell you. You say you don't judge people.

Lilian: You're judging yourself. That's why you're feeling sad, isn't it?

It's not sad! It is utter revulsion, utter revulsion!

Lilian: So, you're judging yourself. Well, that feeling is good, but then there's a time to lose that feeling and turn your life around and start afresh. That's the only way to work your way out of that revulsion and

150

so on. You have to work at it. You know you're sorry for whatever ... and I don't need to know the reason.

SORRY! ... I'll tell you: I can't see you, but I can hear you and I know if you saw me... I'll tell you why I am so revolted with myself, why I can't see a light at the end of the tunnel, why I deserve to be where I am. I killed my child. I ... killed ... my ... child.

<u>Lilian</u>: Right. How old was your child? You can talk about it, if it helps. Can you explain why you did that? *(Pause)* Was the child disabled?

No, no not disabled. My child was ... evil.

<u>Lilian</u>: Yes, I see where you're coming from. How old was the child?

Not a child when I took his life.

<u>Lilian:</u> No, he was grown-up, but he was still your child. And you felt that was the right thing to do.

I could only see more and more evil if I allowed him to continue in the path he was treading. I thought that if I sent him on his way into another life...

<u>Lilian</u>: You realised that he had another life, did you?

Of Course! I also know that I am no longer on the Earth.

<u>Lilian</u>: Good, that's half the battle then, but at the end of the day, you know that that was the wrong thing to do and we really shouldn't kill another human-being, but I do see you *thought* you were doing the right thing at the time.

I thought I would be saving other lives.

<u>Lilian</u>: Yes, I understand. So, did you not tell the police?

In the eyes of the law ... In the eyes of the law, he was an upstanding young man. He was ... he was ... a policeman.

Lilian: He was a policeman himself?

Nobody would have believed me if I'd told them. (I see.) *I watched and I waited, and I watched and I waited, and when I saw what he was doing, I knew I had to act.*

Lilian: But you've had time to think about this now, haven't you? So, you've put yourself in a dark hole and that dark hole shows you that that was the wrong thing to do. I don't know what else you could have done, but there must have been another way. But that's done now and it's gone. Your son's gone and he will know better now, and so do you, otherwise you wouldn't be feeling the way you do.

He was of my flesh and blood and I snuffed his life out like a candle.

Paul: Sometimes, it's better to look at the intention behind the action, rather than the action itself.

Lilian: And pray for him, rather than the way you went. *(I prayed!)* You did?

I still pray for him.

George: Ah! That's very good.

Lilian: Okay. Now you have told us the story of why you're unhappy. I think you're ready to leave all that behind you and go forward in the Spirit world.

George: You used an expression earlier, '*Light at the end of the tunnel*'—there is always that light at the end of the tunnel.

Lilian: You judged yourself. No-one else can judge you, only you. I understand you are a religious person

152

by what you said, but at the end of the day, you are the judge of yourself, only you.

And I judge that I should remain in this darkness.

Lilian: Yes, well now you've thought about it, I think it's time to move forward, because you are just wasting time, aren't you? I think it would be very nice if you could meet your son and work it out for your sake and possibly his as well, but I don't know that ... that you will have to find out as you go forward.

I need to know whether he feels remorse as I do.

Lilian: I'm sure he probably would. At the end of the day, we all do. We all have to face what we've done. We can't escape it

Paul: There's that little spark of goodness in everyone that knows the difference between right and wrong.

He was a good child when he was young.

Lilian: Yes, it happens to a lot of people that they take a wrong turning, a wrong pathway.

He most certainly did that.

Paul: A lot of people, a lot of *very good people* get very lost on the Earth. It's a place where you can really lose yourself and become confused.

Lilian: I think it's time to leave that behind and move forward.

Paul: It's all about learning.

Lilian: Can you not feel love surrounding you and see a light ahead of you?

Oh! The light's been there for a while.

Lilian: Good ... and you need to take a step towards the light, and listen to people on the Spirit side of life that will help you more than I can.

153

They've tried.

Lilian: Yes, well now let them try again.

George: There's Love and there's forgiveness and of course, these are very powerful things to think on.

I will try.

Lilian: Can you see anyone waiting for you in that light?

My son is there. I need time.

Paul: I think this can be turned into a wonderful learning on many levels for both of you. *(General agreement)*

He's getting closer.

Ann: Oh Good!

There are tears on his face.

Paul: Tears of joy, I would imagine.

If they were tears of joy, I would turn from him, but they are tears of remorse, and for that I can walk towards him and take his hand. (Good.) ***Tears of joy would not be appropriate, but they will come in time. Yes, my son ... my son!***

Lilian: Well, we'll let you go and sort things out with your son, and move forward, the pair of you.

George: And into the light!

Let's take another **deep dive** with Salumet, exploring the *balance* of **Light** and **Dark** energy, *paedophilia and* how *restoring balance* holds the *key* to *healing:*

"Yes, my dear friend, those who work within these spheres of work, with these poor Souls, and you must try to see them in that way—again, we come back to judging your fellow man—however *'evil'* they have been, they still are *sparks* of that *Great Creative Divinity.* All eventually must return to the Light—I am moving now into deep, deep matters. All, all energies must return from whence they came, if it takes aeons of time, so be it. But never, never, never, will one Soul be left alone—it will be helped, it will be surrounded by Love, until such time as the Soul can move forward.

When those who bring them to you, use you in your work, you are surrounded by an energy of light, which protects you. I don't think you are fully aware of exactly what happens within the rescues, but each one of you working, would be surrounded by **'*pure energy*,'** which cannot be penetrated by the *darker* elements, because let me tell you, that some of them would try to invade your light. I have spoken briefly too, about *pure energies*, we need to speak about *energy*, rather than *individuals*, to fully understand what is happening. It is why, let me give you an example, why there are those in your world, who would prey upon young children, in a negative way. *(Referring to*

155

paedophiles) **Try to forget the personalities, the age of the people, think wholly on *energy*. And what is happening is this: That young children are mainly '*pure white energy*' and they are preying upon it. Those who have become darkened throughout their lives, are seeking the purity of the white energy. Are you understanding me?**

Les: But they don't realise that that's what they are seeking?

No, it is not, it is *not* purely a physical action, it is an innate feeling that energies must blend, must be whole. And so, they are preying upon this pure energy, which is the child.

Les: So that would be the spark, which you refer to as being in everybody, no matter how '*evil*'—it would be that *spark*, which is trying to find the pure energy?

Yes, all are striving towards being pure energy.

Les: But the physical being is not aware of that?

The physical being would not be aware.

Les: That raises a different aspect ...

That is why it is wrong for you to judge others, without fully realising what lies behind it all."

Salumet 1996/01/29

This is why in *healing prayers* we send *Love* to *ALL* in *spiritual darkness*, to help balance *energies*. *(When doing this work, protection is important before opening ourselves up—see appendix 2.)*

It's good to acknowledge '*wrong-doings*', but not to *lose ourselves* in *judgement*, which adds *negativity*.

Again, the answer comes back to *Love*. If we can accept that there *is* a *Pure Spark of LOVE* in *every*

156

human being, we can allow *Love* and *forgiveness* to work their magic, like in *Spirit rescues*.

Try it—send a bubble of Love to someone you find hard to Love, and notice how it feels—it may take time, but Thoughts of Love will always make a difference.

Psychiatrists and therapists may in future work more with these *spiritual energies* to facilitate *healing*. D*aily meditation* is a great way to *lighten* energies and *restore balance*.

Next, *(2006/03/13)* another in need of *forgiveness*:
<u>Lilian:</u> Can I help you?
Who's there?!
<u>Lilian:</u> It's a friend.
Get out!!
<u>Lilian:</u> Alright, you don't need to be quite so cross.
Get out! Now!
<u>Lilian:</u> Why do you want me to go? Think about it, you don't know my voice, do you?
Get out! I don't want you here, get out! GET OUT!!
<u>Lilian:</u> Why don't you want me here?

I'll do to you what I've done to him if you don't go!
GO!

Lilian: I want you to think about what I'm going to say, you're not in your house, you're in mine.

Not listening; if you don't go, I'll do to you what I've done to him, now go!

Lilian: No, I'm not going to go anyway.

Who are you anyway, who are you?

Lilian: I'm a friend and I'm here to help.

I don't need help.

Lilian: You feel the side of the chair, and you'll find it's not *your* chair, it's a chair of *my* house. *(Pause)*

I hated him, I hated him, I hated him, I hated him…

Lilian: Did you? I wonder if you could forget that for a moment and think about why you're talking to me.

Who the hell are you? Who are you?

Lilian: Good, at last you're beginning to wonder who I am. Well, someone has brought you here, for me to explain what's happened to you. Can you remember…

Don't try and twist words, that won't help…

Lilian: Can you remember having a pain, *(No)* perhaps a bad headache, *(No)* a pain in your chest? *(No)* Nothing?

No, I just felt satisfaction—I hated him, hated, hated, hated him.

Lilian: Okay, well, he's gone, so forget that.

He's not gone, he's there on the bed.

Lilian: Forget about him for a moment and think about yourself. I have to tell you that something has caused you to die.

Tripe!

Lilian: Why do you think you're talking to me...

...because you shouldn't be here—I told you to get out.

Lilian: I'm trying to help you to get to the next life.

You can help me then, help me to get rid of him, help me to get RID of him.

Lilian: You can do *that* if you listen to me.

Go on then, you'll never give me any peace!

Lilian: It's true! *(Chuckles)* Well, you've been brought here for me to do a job and I'm going to do the job...

...and I've told you what the job can be: Help me get rid of him.

Lilian: Well, something has caused you to die and what you have to do is move on into the Spirit world—leave the physical body behind—you are now a Spirit person.

I don't understand all that.

Lilian: Never thought what would happen when you die?

I'm not dead! You're making me angry now!

Lilian: You think you're not, but you ARE. The thing is, you've left the physical body, the body that you had, you've left and that happens to *everybody*—you then take on a Spirit body—go to Heaven, if you want to call it that.

Oh, I knew this would happen, I knew I'd see demons and devils. Who are you, who are you!

Lilian: I'm not a demon or a devil, I'm just plainly telling you what happens.

No, no I don't believe you—I don't believe you.

Lilian: Well, you can now see a bright light in front of you, with someone standing in the light that you should recognise—someone that's died before you.

I told you I don't believe all that rubbish.

Lilian: A mother or a father, can you hear their voice calling you?

Demon voices, demon voices!

Lilian: They're not, that's all your imagination, so put that behind.

What made you so persistent anyway?

Lilian: I told you I've got a job to do.

Who are you?

Lilian: My name is Lilian and you've been sent here to me, because I can help you.

Sent where?

Lilian: You've been sent to me. I've been waiting for you to come.

Well, I said I'd rather be in Hell than live with him—If that's the case—welcome!

Lilian: Well, I think you'll be pleasantly surprised, it won't be Hell, let's say it'll be Heaven—there's no such place as Hell. *(There is)* Only if you want to go to a dark place and you don't want to do that, do you? You want a pleasant life.

That's true. How do you know so much about me anyway, I've never met you?

Lilian: You'd be surprised, but my friends in the Spirit world can tell you a lot more than I can.

Don't keep calling it Spirit world, I don't believe that—don't believe all that stuff.

Lilian: You feel a lot lighter than you used to, don't you? *(Yes)* Well, there you go—why do you feel light? You're also beginning to feel peaceful.
(Voice much calmer now)
I am actually—I feel a bit strange to tell you the truth.
Lilian: You'll get used to it. *(Chuckles)*
I can't leave till I've sorted this out...
Lilian: Can you see anyone yet in the light?
No, I can hear voices, but I ain't gonna be talking to them.
Lilian: Who was the person you were most fond of?
My mother.
Lilian: There you are then, she'll be waiting.
Not convinced, but I do feel strange—very strange in fact.
Lilian: I'm ever so glad you've listened to me.
That doesn't mean I've taken any notice, but I do feel a bit odd. Where's he gone to now? Who's taken him, who's taken him?
Lilian: Don't worry about that, I want you to concentrate on your mother.
My dear old mother—oh God, I can see her. Oh my God!
Lilian: She's smiling at you.
She's beckoning to me.
Lilian: Probably saying come on, you should be listening.
I can't believe it's true.
Lilian: Well, it is true. In other words, we cannot really die, can we?
That scares me.

161

Lilian: Put all that behind you and just go forward and enjoy life again.

Oh my God, she's getting closer.

Lilian: Happy to go?

I'm not sure. It looks like her…It's not the demons in my head, is it?

Lilian: They'll soon go. If you go with your mother, you'll find they'll all go.

Okay—if I come back, watch out. (Chuckles)

Lilian: I'm just pleased to have been able to help you.

In this next rescue, (1994/08/29) *Salumet participates*. It involves one who found it particularly hard to *forgive himself.* Leslie encourages him to speak, giving reassurances that there would be no *criticism* or *judgement*—Salumet joins at this point:

You are forgiven my son—you are forgiven.

Les: Thank you. I knew he was wanting forgiveness. God bless you, now you can be happy, now you can face the world. You heard what was said, you are forgiven.

(Spoken loudly) I heard.

Les: Good, that's fine.

(Spoken with great compassion) **Speak to us, my son. Let it come from the heart. Let yourself be**

free. We *Love* you, we want to *help* you. Speak to us.

I didn't mean to do it.

We know—all we want is to embrace you in our *Love* and our *Light*. But first you need to learn to *forgive yourself,* forgive *yourself*—it is the hardest thing that you must do. But we *Love* you my son. You are surrounded by much, much Love, but don't you see, you cannot go forward until that forgiveness is given to *yourself.*

<u>Les:</u> You can make amends if that's what you wish, by helping many, many others.

I wish to go with the others.

<u>Les:</u> You can go with the others, once you have done as you were asked, forgive yourself. Then you can go with them—they'll accept you. But *they* can't make *you* forgive yourself—that is something *you* have to do.

It is very hard.

<u>Les:</u> Of course it is, that's why you've been brought here tonight, for us to offer help, to assist you to do it, but we can't do it for you.

There is something he wishes to ask, but he is afraid—don't be afraid of me my son, ask what you will, I will endeavor to help all that I can. What is it you wish to ask me? *Don't* be afraid.

It is difficult.

<u>Les:</u> Of course it is, we understand that, but we can't ask it for you. Give yourself the pleasure of asking, will you, then you can go with the others. Isn't it worth it, if you want to follow them and go with them?

163

You want to help, don't you? *(Yes.)* Yes. Are those words too difficult for you to say to me? It is what we have waited to hear from you; the desire, the wish to help others. *That* is what you want, is it not?

That is correct.

But first, my son, we need to show you a little more of yourself, before you can do that. By speaking *with us*, to us, by asking to be forgiven, you have taken that *first step.* Now I say to you, go with those who have brought you. And I can say this to you with an open heart, you *will be guided* by those who *Love* you, who want to *help* you, and you can take it *one* step at a time from there.

Les: You understand? *(I do.)* Good.

May God's blessings be with you, encourage you, help you and give you the Love you need to sustain you. God bless you my son. Now *go, go* with those who brought you. *(Pause)*

Les: You walk backwards to go forwards.

Salumet commented afterwards:

There are so many of these souls who find it so difficult to forgive themselves. They think their transgressions are worse than anything that could be known. Of course, they are wrong. We only want to help and to Love them, but sometimes they imprison themselves in their *own prison*— again the *POWER* of *THOUGHT*...

The **Power of** *Thought* is the *heart-core* of the *Salumet teachings.* This *Spiritual Truth* is well rooted in history. The *strength* and *positivity* of *Mahatma Gandhi*'s THINKING helped him become a *light* for

164

Peaceful Change in the world, illustrating the *Power* of *Love and Forgiveness*. Likewise with *rescue work,* when *Love and forgiveness flow,* the right *Conditions for Transformation* are possible. As soon as *judgement* comes into play, *energetic conditions* deteriorate and this is also the case with *real change* in the world. *Love and forgiveness* open the doors to *real change—hatred and fear* keep them closed *tight.* Gandhi could *Love and forgive oppressors*, helping to create the conditions for *world changing transformation*!

Similarly, *Nelson Mandela* imprisoned and tortured for *27 years,* still managed to keep going positively, helping to *peacefully* end *apartheid* in *South Africa*, taking a giant step towards what *Paul McCartney* and *Stevie Wonder sang about: 'Ebony and Ivory living in perfect harmony...'* ♫ ♫ ♫ These 2 *truly honourable peacemakers, (Not Paul and Stevie, though they're really cool too!)* were *labelled 'terrorists'* by western governments and mainstream media *(MSM).*
J.K.Rowling's books brilliantly illustrate how this works, when *'The Daily Prophet' aligns* itself to the *'Dark Lord'* and *bombards Dumbledore* and *Harry Potter* with untrue and divisive headlines. *MSM* is similarly not immune to the influence of *dark Lords*—or maybe we should call them: *'Lords who need a bit more Love and Light'.* Even the *Suffragettes* were treated more like *terrorists* than woman striving *for fairness* and *equality.*
So the next time someone is *attacked in the media,* it's wise to *question* whether they *really* are

'baddies', or courageous *people* like the Suffragettes, *Gandhi, Mandela.*

It's intriguing to specuate how *MSM* and governments would *describe* Jesus[9] today? Turning water into wine and feeding people would be wonderful, but healing the sick could bring conflict with *Big Pharma*—and what if he told people they didn't need a certain vaccination or encouraging *ceasefires* not war? It could soon turn into another *witch-hunt,* unless things *lighten up* on this planet. *Loving thoughts* may not sound like much of a *revolutionary remedy*, but Salumet encourages us in this direction, explaining that *THOUGHTS* are a *living ENERGY* and *WE* are *ENERGY*. It makes sense when you think how easily a flashlight lightens up the dark, so *imagine* what would happen if everyone started *shining spiritual flashlights, or Wands of Love* upon 'dark lords'- negative media - governments? It could be like the *wonderful transformation* of *Ebenezer Scrooge* on Christmas Day! *('A Christmas Carol' by Charles Dickens)*

"I cannot stress to you too much how important *THOUGHT* is. Thought, *THOUGHT* is the most *powerful thing* that you possess."
Salumet 1994/09/12

---

[9] For more ideas on how Jesus might be treated today, listen to the song *'The Ballad of Peter Pumpkinhead'*, by XTC

In the next rescue, *(2022/01/31)* as usual we didn't know the full picture, but we usually find the right words, thanks to Spirit:

Eileen: Does anyone want to talk?

No.

Paul: Well, you've been brought here, so it would be very good if you could talk to us, *(No)* because we *can* help you. And I think you know you need a bit of help. We are here to do that for you. Just the fact that you've come here, is a wonderful *change*, which I'm sure you can begin to feel already—a little bit of warmth and maybe a bit more *peace* than you've felt for a while. We don't need to know too many details, but we can help you on your way. Do you know what's happened to you?

I lost my arms.

Paul: Yeah, and do you know what happens when— we call it 'death', but...

I can't find them anywhere.

Paul: Well, in fact that caused you to die, but do you know what happens *after* you die? Do you have a belief in Heaven, or something like that?

Not like that.

Paul: Most people don't quite understand, and it's the sort of thing you can't fully understand until you finally *get there*, but the fact is, it *does exist* and it's as good as anyone can imagine it to be and it's time for you to experience it. At some point we all have to and I expect—can you see any kind of little light or something very bright?

No, I don't deserve it.

Paul: That's what a lot of people say, it's funny, but that's like a religion talking, but actually we *ALL* go there—everybody goes there, because it's where we all *came from*, they call it '*going Home*,' it's like going to your *true HOME* and there's nothing undeserving, because the Earth is actually a place to *learn*. So, it's okay to make mistakes on Earth—everybody makes mistakes, it's about the *learning*, and when it's time to go, you've had your life, you go back to '*Heaven*' and yes, there will be a chance to improve on the things you didn't do so well, but you're not *judged* for it, not by other people. As I say, it's a *learning planet* for everyone.

I don't want to see her, tell her to go!

Paul: There are lots of people who'll want to see you—you don't *have to* see anyone once you go to '*Heaven*'—freewill still exists—you can choose to see who you wish. Is there anyone you'd like to see—a grandparent or someone who's already gone? *(No!)* Well, you don't have to. Some people even get lots of help and healing from an animal that you've grown to like … you may see someone or perhaps an animal, when you see this *Light*.

My mother is there and I don't want to see her.

Paul: Whatever experience you *had* with your mother it's *already changed*.

No, you don't understand. I did something very wrong—I don't deserve her Love.

Paul: Well, it sounds crazy, but *EVERYTHING does get forgiven*—everything can be *forgiven*.

No, not this.

Sara: But she wouldn't be there if she hadn't forgiven you.

Paul: Because we don't really 'die'—we *can't* really die—there's so much we don't realise on Earth. Take one step at a time, but you can ask your mother to stay, or if you don't feel you wish to see her right now—but if she's come, she really wants you to know she's still got the Love for you.

Sara: And that is normal for mothers to have unconditional Love, it's the highest and natural way for them to feel. So, it's maybe that you just need to forgive yourself and then you can accept her forgiveness.

Paul: She can tell you how to make amends, if you feel you have to… Is she still there? *(Mm)* So, I think she still really wishes for you to…it's never as simple as it seems—you'll see that our lifetimes have many other aspects—everything is a *learning experience*, even terrible wars, they're looked on slightly differently when we get to *Heaven*, get to *Spirit;* you will see that much learning takes place, in ways we can't foresee.

Yes, I see that.

Paul: The fact that she's there means something. She can help you and maybe you can *still help her* as well.

Sara: She would love you to accept her *Love.*

Paul: I know it seems a big step going back, but you can do it, you can do it. *(Mm)*

Eileen: Give her the name *'Sheila'* Paul—who's a sister.

<u>Paul:</u> Sheila is here—much more *Love* for you than you realise and it's all there ahead of you in that *light*. *(Thank you.)*

Sabine explained afterwards that he was a suicide bomber too ashamed to see his mother.

<u>Salumet on the Love of a parent for a child:</u>

"It is the *purest of energy*—think of the mother with the new-born child and you can feel the expression of that *unconditional Love.*"

"There should be *unconditional Love* for all your fellow men, of course. That is why the *mother's Love* for a child is so great, because it is *unconditional.* If only mankind could feel that kind of *Love* for his fellow man, then this planet would be a much, much better place."

Salumet 2001/07/23 and 2006/11/27

Imagine this deep Love enfolding the whole of humanity, regardless of whatever labels they are given, just unconditionally loving ALL ...
Powerful Magic!

Next, *(2021/12/06)* a traumatic rescue of one who had made a *pact* with her partner to hang themselves—but her partner didn't go through with it:

You lied to me! *(Confusion at first ....)*

<u>Paul:</u> Oh, not intentionally, I'm sorry if that seemed the case.

You coward, you lied to me!

<u>Paul:</u> Can I just ask where do you think you are now? I think we might be a bit confused—what's the last thing you remember?

Opening my eyes.

<u>Paul:</u> And where were you when you opened your eyes?

Hanging on the tree.

<u>Paul:</u> Ah, I understand now the confusion. You've been brought *here*—we can help you.

No, you lied to me, you lied to me!

<u>Paul:</u> Well, I don't know who lied to you, but my name's Paul and you've been brought here and we can help you. I'm not the one you think I am perhaps, but we're here to help—you're amongst friends now. Whatever you did, whatever happened, that's the past now, we've got to move forward.

No, no we don't, you lied and lied.

<u>Paul:</u> Someone perhaps lied to you, I can understand if that happened—someone lied—you'll have time to decide what to do about it later, but now we need to check you're okay, because we're here to help. Are you beginning to feel better now? You should be beginning to feel better—the healing should be

starting—it works pretty fast. You should be feeling a bit warmer.

Who are you?

Paul: My name's Paul and I'm here to help. So, I suspect you know what's happened? Everybody dies at some point and some people realise that we don't *really 'die'*, we actually continue, our *Souls*, our *Spirits* continue.

He said we'd be together forever—he lied!

Paul: Well actually … when we die, which is what's happened to you, *we do* go to a place a bit like *Heaven* and we *do* get to see all the loved ones that have passed already. So, anyone that's passed, perhaps your parents, perhaps old friends, uncles, aunties, anybody—even old pets, beloved animals—they're all there, waiting for us. You can reunite with them—It will all be explained, it sounds probably a bit *too good to be true*, but I can promise you that this is where we *all* go, to a wonderful place of *Love and healing*.

Why didn't he love me? Why? *(Tearful)*

Paul: It will be made clear to you, someone will explain why that is the case, but *the main thing to remember is YOU ARE LOVED*, and you'll find lots of people who *will Love YOU,* amazingly *deeply.* This one wasn't for whatever reason, but it will all be explained. There is so much Love waiting and you should be able to see a light in front of you.

I can.

Paul: Wonderful! This light, it's like a *Tunnel of Love* and you may even recognise someone—an old familiar face in the light.

172

My mama—mama.

Paul: Ah, I'm sure she's got a lot of Love for you and she'll explain and take care of you.

Thank you for your help.

Paul: It's a pleasure to help and I'm so pleased you can now be on your way, *'back Home'*, as we call it.

What are you called?

Paul: I'm Paul—maybe we'll get to meet one day, again.

Yes—I'm sorry.

Paul: That's fine—you had a difficult time, but you'll be fine.

Let's take another **deep dive** with *Salumet* into the *deep, deep waters* of *suicide* and *euthanasia*. These are *highly emotive* subjects and as always, accept only that which you *feel* is right and place to one side anything that seems *unacceptable to you:*

<u>Q and A session (2012/01/16):</u>

Sarah: There's been a lot of discussion about *euthanasia*. They're not going to do it through the *Power of Thought,* so they go to clinics to end their *lives*—I wonder if you're able to tell us a little more about why we shouldn't do that?

Because you are curtailing your life before your lifespan is finished. Why should you curtail that lifespan, because you think it is right, or you are right? You do not see the wider picture, once again. So therefore, why do you feel it is right to

173

curtail that life? It is not correct—It is *never* right, and I will stress *NEVER right.*

Jan: In no circumstance whatsoever is it right—is that what you're saying?

When the Spirit is ready, they will go naturally.

Jan: So, no matter how much *pain* and *discomfort* they are in, that is where they have to be at that particular time? **(Yes)** Even if they were to touch one more life while they were in that despair…

Yes—very often, in the *time of discomfort*, does the *Spirit come to the fore?*

Jan: It seems to *soar*, doesn't it?

Yes, and although I understand that human beings find this distressing, and so often we hear: we would not allow animals—and I understand that Love that you have, but you do not have the right to shorten your own lives. You can use your mind to help you along, but it should be a natural end.

Jan: So, with an elderly domestic animal?

Animals apply to the rules of the human beings on this Earth. Yes, they belong to *Spirit* in the same way that you do. So, I would say 'no'.

George: It's very good to have your firm statement Salumet—there's been much discussion in the media.

Yes, there is much controversy I know, but always I have to say that is where I stand—that is what I know.

Rod: Would you agree that if some people get into a deep black hole of depression and within a couple of days, they hang themselves—I can only think that something terrible happened in the *brain* to do this when they leave *children* and a *wife*…

174

Of course, my dear friend, but that still does not make it right. We know all of these things are part of earthly living. We see it all so often and you would be amazed at how many tears are shed in Spirit for these beings who suffer so in that way, but it still is not part of *'Universal Law'*. I have to say and I know that some people become upset and offended when I say that suicide is the most selfish of acts.

<u>Jan:</u> It is—without judging them—it is! **(Yes)**

<u>Rod:</u> Somebody said that to me recently that was a *selfish act*—I said: you can't say that—but he was right!

No, it is a selfish act and also—often, I only wish you could see the despair they feel at what they've done.

<u>Rod:</u> When they go over? **(Yes.)**

<u>Jan:</u> You can't turn back.

You cannot run away from a life given.

<u>George:</u> Can I indicate a special type of suicide undertaken by some Tibetan monks who deliberately torch themselves in protest? It's a *political act*, so in that sense it's *not* selfish—how would you regard that Salumet?

In a way, I understand what you are saying, but it *is selfish* that they deprive those who have loved them of that Love. Remember: *Love is everything* and just to hurt deliberately one human being can never be accepted. No-one on this planet is a sole-entity. All of you are intertwined in one way or another, be it to a husband, a wife, to children, to parents—no-one stands alone. So, I have to say yes

175

it would still be considered as a selfish act, although, as I say, I understand that *they feel* it is unselfish. Their view will change when their whole picture is once again shown to them. I cannot deviate from this answer, because it is the Truth.

Salumet 2012/01/16

Salumet also suggests that sometimes our loved ones and beloved pets *hang on* longer than necessary, due to the sadness they *sense in us*, even though they are *ready* to *'let go'*. It can be helpful to give **'Permission to go'**, so that they will *transition naturally*, with the understanding that *we* will be *alright*.

In that sense, *'Live and let **die**'* is *good*, though perhaps we should leave **'licences to kill'** to *God/Great Creative Force*. Sorry *Mr Bond*, but you can always be reassigned to *Spiritual Service— licence to HEAL.*

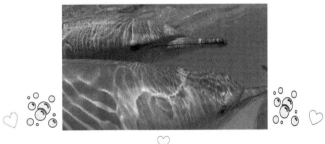

Related links:

Salumet on Depression:

http://www.salumetandfriends.org/app/download/1 2221587/Salumet+on+Depression.pdf

Salumet on Suicide:

https://www.salumet.org/80-suicide
Salumet on Abortion:
http://www.salumetandfriends.org/app/download/1
2221589/Salumet+on+Abortion.pdf
'The Forgiveness Project' is a charity encouraging forgiveness, with victims and perpetrators coming together to help heal.

Though this next one is *not a rescue, (2013/12/02)* the visitor shares *her story* about *forgiveness*, viewed with wisdom and hindsight from *Spirit world*—we don't suddenly become *all-knowing* when we leave the human stage, but we do see more:

This isn't easy you know. *(We've been told many times, it's not as easy as some seem to think, being channelled through a medium.)*

Lilian: I'm sure it's not. Yes, we're told that quite often.

I can't believe they say it's easy!

Lilian: Some people come quite a bit. Is this your first time?

Yes, I tried to speak with my sister. She couldn't hear me, so I was given permission to come to you. Is that okay?

Lilian: Yes, that's fine. Were you just curious that it could be done?

A little, but I have something to say—something that's held me back for quite some time: 'Forgiveness'.

Lilian: You mean: to forgive yourself? *(Yes)* That must be very hard. *(It is—very hard.)* We all know when we've done wrong.

I did not do wrong—I just could not forgive.

Lilian: Oh, you couldn't forgive someone else!

Yes, why should I? That was my question—why should I forgive?

Lilian: Yes, it's hard, but it's better for you if you can.

I understand that now. So, I wanted to come and say: please, every one of you look inside yourselves, and if you have any 'unforgiveness' in your being, to let it go—please, please—it destroys you.

George: Yes, these are wise words—true words *(yes)*—a good message, thank you.

Yes, I would not like anyone to suffer the way that I have.

George: We have political deeds and violence on our planet at times and it's so easy to not forgive that *(yes)*, but ultimately, we must, I think you will agree.

Yes, forgiveness for whatever reason. Mine, I have to tell you, was more personal.

Lilian: Something to do with your sister? If it's upsetting, I wouldn't talk about it.

It still upsets me, but I know myself—I know better now.

Sara: Some things are very testing though, aren't they? You probably had something extremely testing.

She stole my husband—how could I forgive her?

Sara: Yes exactly, that's hard. That's very, very difficult, because it's close family as well as a

178

betrayal and it's very difficult. So, I can understand if you struggled with that.

But you do not realise what unforgiveness does unless you have suffered it.

Lilian: Not to that extent—It must have been very hard for you.

It was, but it was within my power to change my way of thinking. How could I not forgive her? That was the question I struggled with for so long. But please, all of you, think carefully about any situation in your lives where unforgiveness rears its head, because you are the ones who would suffer, not the person that you direct this unforgiveness to.

Sara: Did you suffer a lot in your earthly life then, by carrying the unforgiveness?

Towards the end I became quite ill and it was only when I came here that I realised that it was the thoughts of unforgiveness which had caused the problems. So, I suffered but still I could not forgive, until I came here.

George: The one who comes here to teach, he says exactly this. He also says: we must forgive the past, and that is very important.

You must forgive YOURSELF, you have to …

Lilian: I imagine, in the long run, your sister and ex-husband, needed to forgive *THEM*selves.

Yes, I have had no contact. I tried to speak with my sister but she could not hear me now.

Lilian: It's just a case of waiting for a reunion in Spirit.

It is. I have to thank you for allowing me to speak. Although I became a little upset, I am no longer upset. It is only when I return, at first, I begin to get that feeling…

Lilian: Yet there must be a lesson there somewhere for everyone.

That is why I wanted to tell someone. I have carried this with me for too long, and it is like a release of some kind. It is almost like your mind is free of all of that hatred and unforgiveness.

Lilian: Yes, it's a hard one though…

But, as long as you are aware that these things can happen, you can change how you FEEL and how you THINK…

This chapter has *touched* on *some* deep subjects and to lighten the mood, this isn't a rescue, but the lady needed to return to have some final *earthly laugher*. It begins *(2009/06/08)* with Eileen muttering quietly, *'I just want to laugh'*—her shoulders started moving up and down, followed by *ripples of laughter:*

Lilian: Hello. *(More raucous laughing)* What do you find funny?

Oh dearie! *(More infectious laughter)*

Lilian: Are you going to tell us what's making you laugh so much?

(Further giggles)—I died laughing!

Lilian: When? *(Sighs)*

Paul: That's a good way to go, I guess!

Sarah: It's cheered us all up! *(Agreed) (More laughs)*

Lilian: Did you think we were rather a sullen lot?

George: The last time I heard laughter like that was in a Laurel and Hardy movie, where Stan Laurel was being tickled.

180

*(More chuckles)—**Can't help it dearie.***

<u>Lilian</u>: No, I don't think you can!

You thought I was joking, didn't you? I DID die laughing!

<u>Lilian</u>: Oh, you died '*laughing*'—I thought you said, '*last week*'! *(Lilian's hearing isn't always good)*

(More guffaws of laughter)

<u>Lilian</u>: A nice way to go! ***(Yes—bit of a shock!)*** I can imagine!

Yes—This one's saying, hurry up and go, you're making me ache*! (Referring to the medium, Eileen)*

<u>Lilian</u>: So, how long have you been over in the Spirit world?

God only knows! *(More hearty laughs!)*

<u>Lilian</u>: Does it seem a long time?

*(Further chortles)—**I must stop it now—they're saying, 'Just settle down'.** (Pause) **I've stopped now.***

<u>Sarah</u>: I wonder why you've come to visit us, if you came with your laughter, to cheer us all up, or if you came to tell us something?

Nothing to tell you.

<u>Sarah</u>: Isn't there? So, do you laugh a lot in Spirit?

Well, I just needed to do it one last time—re-live what happened, you know? But, I'm quite happy about it. I don't mind…

<u>Lilian</u>: But you were a giggler, while you were in this life, were you?

Laughing too much and had a heart-attack.

<u>Rod</u>: Were you watching something, to make you laugh?

No, I was with my friends—friends all laughing together.

181

Lilian: Having a good laugh.

Sarah: And then you had a heart-attack? *(Yes.)*

Lilian: So, they probably all stopped laughing.

Yes—anyway.

Sarah: So, were you very old? *(54.)* Not desperately old. *(No)* Well, I would say that's a very good way to go. *(Yes)*

Lilian: So, it was a surprise for you, that obviously it was very quick?

Well, I believed in an afterlife anyway, but they just said, come back, get it out the way, then you can carry on, carry on with your life. So, as soon as I came back, I saw this lady, (Eileen) and thought, I'll choose her. I've had a look all round tonight!

Sarah: You weren't too frightened by us all then?

You all seemed very quiet and relaxed...

Lilian: We're not always so quiet. *(No?)*

George: Well, we get quite a mixture here, we have some serious teaching, but we also enjoy a laugh!

Good—everyone should laugh, shouldn't they? (Agreed) Anyway, I must go—got to go. Thank you all very much for your time—I definitely feel better!

Chapter 9

Illnesses and Disabilities

*P*hysical bodies can be compared to *Avatars*—our chosen *instruments,* interfaced and controlled by our *Spirit selves*, until too old or damaged/kaput/knackered/no longer *operational— like a dead parrot?*

When the *physical body* dies, the *memory* of a condition may persist in the *etheric body,* which is the body we inhabit after the *physical* body stops working. Once **Home,** our *etheric bodies* can be easily healed in the loving care of *Spirit Hospitals/Temples of Healing.*

Switching from the *physical* to the *etheric*, is perhaps like having an *Avatar upgrade.* The famous ***ABBA avatars*** can *dance, sing* and *leap around on stage,* just like in the *golden years* of ABBA—though the group are now *elders*—though *still just as beautiful!* In Spirit world, our *etheric bodies* can perform *even better* than *ABBA Avatars,* allowing *full health* and a return to *our golden years* and so much more—*a wonderful **voyage** awaits!*

The gentleman in this rescue had been on *life-support*, without movement for *many years* and was now unable to move forward—definitely ready for his '*Avatar upgrade*'. One began via Paul, while another gave assistance via Jan:

I can't bring myself to say it.

<u>Jan:</u> *What do you want to say?*

I am not ready to say it.

<u>Jan:</u> *No? Well, it would help you.*

It's too early.

<u>Lilian</u>: Can you give us a name?

I am Harry. *(General welcomes)*

<u>Jan:</u> *These people are nice people—that's why I brought them to you—or you to them.*

It's not their fault.

<u>Jan:</u> *No, no, but if you are able to open up to these people. It will help you.*

I am so frustrated with myself, but I can't do this.

<u>Jan:</u> *Well, this is a great opportunity for you. How can these people help you then? Would you like to feel the physical touch on your hand again—would that help? You've come such a long way.*

I haven't got the ability.

<u>Jan:</u> *You DO have the ability! We all do have the ability, you do—and you have the conviction to do this. This is your healing and you need to try to find everything you have to do this. We can try this again and again and again.*

I was not able to do much when I was here before.

<u>Lilian:</u> Were you disabled? *(Yes.)* You know you're okay now.

Jan: He doesn't believe it, that's the thing. He has the conviction, but he doesn't believe what we're telling him.

I want to believe it.

Lilian: You want to believe you're okay.

I'm having a lot of help, I know.

Lilian: Where-abouts were you disabled?

I was completely without movement.

Jan: If it helps, I can explain. Harry was in what was called an 'Iron lung'. They don't have those now. So, all Harry looked at was a mirror.

Lilian: Yeah—that was tough. I think you're ready to go out and explore, don't you?

I feel that I could do something.

Lilian: Yeah—you feel you'd be lost without the— where you were, with the Iron-lung.

I want to move, but I can't.

Lilian: Well, let's see what we can do.

Sarah: Did you have a sister?

I had a sister, yes.

Sarah: I think your sister is with me and she's trying to help you. So, if you try and imagine that she's sitting next to you—she's putting her hand out and wants you to put your hand out—and I know you couldn't, but you can _now_. Try just putting your hand forward.

Lilian: Come on, I'll help you—you can feel the warmth in my hands. Just gently try putting it up a little bit. Okay? Tell me if you want me to stop.

Sarah: And when you've done that, you're going to be able to do all the other things, because now you know you _can_.

185

(Harry gradually began moving fingers and arms.)

<u>Sarah:</u> So now your sister is going to stand by you, until you totally believe that you can be whole again. It was that first step you needed to take.

<u>Sara:</u> Well done Harry!

<u>Graham:</u> How long was he in the Iron-lung for?

<u>Jan:</u> *All of his life—from 6-months old.*

<u>Sarah:</u> There isn't any Iron-lung there now.

<u>Lilian:</u> No, that's fading away.

<u>Sarah:</u> The sister has gone back now and is waiting for you.

<u>Jan:</u> *How does that feel now Harry? You've made the first step, haven't you?*

Yes, I can feel the body moving.

<u>Jan:</u> *No fear, take the fear away—it's only the fear that stops you from moving—doesn't need to exist anymore.*

I feel like I'm ready to fly! *(Congratulations and chuckles)*

<u>Sarah:</u> We're really happy for you.

<u>Jan:</u> *We're gonna fly back then!*

<u>Sarah:</u> When you get back, your sister's going to be there, waiting for you. And you can run and jump and all the other things you want to do. **(Yes!)**

<u>Jan:</u> *We'll go the long way round and fly!* **(I really am ready.)** *There you go, that's brilliant!* **(Thank you everyone!)**

186

Next, *(2006/05/29)* a *drug-addict* needing a helping hand:

Lilian: Feeling a bit lost and miserable? Can you tell me what is wrong? If I put my hands on your back, you'll begin to feel a lovely warmth coming through, which will help you to talk to me.

(Lilian continued to reassure the person, who seemed in too much pain to articulate audible speech.)

Stop the pain, stop the pain!

Lilian: That's why I've got my hand on your back. I want you to think about this carefully: The pain is beginning to go. You don't need that pain anymore. Think about it…

I'm so cold!

Lilian: Yes, I know—okay?

(The person continues to be in pain and Lilian persists that the pain is going.)

I need it, I need it, I need it! I need it, I need it, I need it!

Lilian: You don't need the pain, you *think* you do, but you *don't* need the pain at all.

I'm so cold…

Lilian: Warmth is coming all around you. I'll explain why you don't need the pain or the cold: Something caused you to die, which means you leave the physical body behind and you take on a brand-new body in the Spirit world/the next world. And with that brand-new body, you'll have no more pain, no cold and you'll have friends waiting for you, saying: *"Come on, why are you hanging about"?* You see, you're relaxing now—feeling better? Someone's calling for you? Can you hear someone calling your name?

(Now the mind seemed clearer.) **Where am I? Where am I?**

Lilian: You're in my house and I'm just telling you what's happened to you. Don't worry about it.

I don't know where I am...

Lilian: All the pain's gone? *(Yes)* Good—you're surprised, aren't you? *(I am)* I think there's someone waiting to take you with them—someone that you know.

I don't know...

Lilian: There will be—look towards the bright Light. Someone there is waiting for you, you only needed someone to tell you what had happened to you, so that you could get rid of the pain.

Yeah, yeah, I see it, I see it! Yeah.

Lilian: Happy to go?

Yeah—I want to go, want to go, yeah—got to go...

In this world as in *Spirit realm, help is* always available—just waiting to be asked …

"You must send your Love to all things upon the planet; it is not the only planet which is going through some trauma, but you must always be *hopeful*, you must always be *positive,* because if only you could see the brightness of your spiritual lights, I have said this on many occasions, but I

188

feel I need to reiterate it, you must always *think brightly* with good thoughts and *know,* not just hope, *KNOW THAT ALL WILL BE WELL."*

Salumet 2020/01/13

This next one *(2006/05/01)* appears to have a *multiple personality disorder*, hence the use of *different fonts* to illustrate two personalities:

Lilian: Good evening.

I would like to twist your ears off!

Lilian: Yes! *(Chuckles…thinking it was a bit of a joke)*

Don't you laugh at me!

Lilian: It's better to laugh than cry, isn't it? I'm not laughing *at* you—that would be unkind.

I'd like to twist your ears off. Where am I?

Lilian: You're in my house and I'm hoping to be able to help you.

You can't help me—YOU can't help me!

Lilian: Why is that?

I won't be locked up anymore, I won't I won't I WON'T be locked up anymore!

Lilian: No, I can assure you, you won't. Does that help, I can assure you, you won't be locked up anymore.

(Two guttural shrieking noises)

Lilian: Don't you believe me? You just said you don't want to be locked up—I can assure you that you won't be.

(Desperate whimpering and the words 'Go away' followed by a different sounding voice saying 'I won't go away'—like a multiple personality)

189

Lilian: We're here to help you.

SHE can't make me go away!

Lilian: I want you to listen to me: You've been brought here so that we can talk to you, me and my friends, because something has caused you to die and what you have to do, is to start living in the Spirit world. Does that sound strange? You don't need to start thumping your hands up and down, because it's perfectly true. *(Arms moving agitatedly)* That's why you're free, you can move on and look forward to a decent life, only not on the Earth.

Whimpering voice: ***I want to be free, I want to be free!***

Lilian: You ARE free—listen: You ARE FREE—it doesn't matter what you've done or what others have done, you're free NOW.

...Don't let them do that...

Lilian: No, they won't they've gone, they've gone.

She's stupid! She's stupid!

Lilian: Never mind about that, think about yourself now, *just* yourself. You're free and you're ready to move on—away from the life that you didn't like.

(In a calmer voice): ***They said I'm mad—I'm not mad, I'm not mad.***

Lilian: I know you're not mad.

She keeps coming—I don't know who I am, I don't know who I am, help me, help me please, help me.

Lilian: That's why you're here. What's your name? Can you tell me your name? *(Peter.)* Peter, that's a nice name—hello Peter. I want you to just think about yourself for the moment—forget about all that's gone on in your life, you have to move on.

I want to be helped—I want to be helped.

Lilian: Good, that's what we're waiting for—you want to be helped. Now, what can you see ahead of you? You should see a nice bright light and a lovely feeling surrounding you. My friends are there waiting to help you.

I hear music—music.

Lilian: Good! You liked music, didn't you? Where you're going, you can have all the music you want. *(Please...)* A friend of mine is waiting to take you by the hand and help you. Will you go with that friend of mine? You've listened to me and I'm sure you'll listen to my friend.

I'm scared, I'm really so scared.

Lilian: You don't need to be scared, though it's strange, I'm sure, but you're going *HOME*, to the best *Home* you'll ever have.

They won't lock me away again?

Lilian: You have friends around you.

Paul: No, they won't lock you away.

Rod: That's all finished with—that's all gone.

I can see, I can see some arms...

Lilian: Waiting to help you.

Please come with me, you'll come with me, you help me...

Lilian: You can still hear the music?

I feel like I've never felt before.

Lilian: Peace? *(Peace...)* Peace and Love.

Peace and Love.

Sarah: That's good—lovely.

I want to go.

Sarah: Yes—take hold of that arm that's holding out…

Lilian: Yeah, you take hold of the arm.

It's beautiful! It's beautiful!

Beautiful music can provide *wonderful healing,* both here and in Spirit world. Salumet explains that there is also great healing in *birdsong:*

"Not only is the dawn chorus from the birds of your world, they are accompanied by the Angelic Beings in our world, which, if only you could be aware, you would see the strength and energy and how the Earth can be transmuted from darkness to light. It is a whole choir of not only the physical birds and energies of the world, but also from our world; they are united, they are in unison with the vibration of sound. And I would say to you that sometimes when people are ready to return *home* to us, they will often say they hear music; that is part of the changes that are made within your world by those of us in Spirit. It is a sound, an energy that is more beautiful than you could be aware of here. But yes, that dawn chorus, as it has been named, is a most beautiful happening within your world and within ours."

Salumet 2016/09/12

The next one *(2023/04/17)* seemed to have *learning difficulties*:

One, two, buckle my shoe.

192

Paul/Eve: Three, four, knock on my door.

No, no, no: One, two, buckle my shoe—one, two, buckle my shoe. Do-pe-doon?

Paul: Ah, that's a nice little rhythm, isn't it? *(Doop-doon.)* Doop-doom? *(Doop-doon!)* Doop-doon, yeah…

One-two, buckle my shoe, buckle my shoe, buckle my shoe.

Paul: So, when did you learn that rhythm?

No, no, no—go away, go away. One-two, buckle my shoe, one-two, buckle my shoe.

Paul: It's a nice little rhythm though…

Mm, have some zoop-zoon?

Paul: Ah, some soup? Do you want some?

Yes—one-two…

Paul: If you look ahead of you, I think there might be a lady bringing you some zoop-zoom.

Zoop-zoom.

Paul: Can you see someone ahead of you? *(Yes.)* Is it a lovely lady?

It's you!

Chuckles

Paul: Is it me? Oh! Well, and can you see the zoop-zoom?

I like the zoop-zoom-zoom. One-two…I'm not mad, I'm not mad.

Paul: No, I know you're not, I know you're not. I think there's a place for you to go and if you want some zoop-zoom…

Zoop-zoom…boon, spoon. Soup-spoon…

Paul: Yes, you'll need a spoon to eat your soup-zoom, and I think there is someone—can you *feel*

193

someone, or look at someone that is ahead of you, that's got a spoon for you? Can you see a little bright light ahead of you?

Mm, I'm not mad.

<u>Paul:</u> I know you're not, I know you're not. It's just that I think someone is bringing something for you, but you just need to look ahead of you.

Bringing zoup?

<u>Paul:</u> Yes, bringing zoup for you. Can you see a light ahead of you—a lady bringing a spoon and a zoup? You may even be able to smell it?

Mm, nice, nice.

<u>Paul:</u> Can you smell it? *(Yes.)* It's just ahead of you, so if you follow that lady, follow that light, maybe she'll reach out and you can hold her hand and she'll probably have the spoon as well. So, if you… *(Mm)* She's a lovely lady…

Yeah—there she is, there she is.

<u>Paul:</u> Got her?

One-two, buckle my shoe…

<u>Paul:</u> So, she'll look after you, she'll give you your zoup. Can you feel yourself going towards her? *(Mm)* You can kind of float towards her really.

Mm, she's warm.

<u>Paul:</u> Mm, a warm and a real peace—a beautiful peace.

Yeah—I'm not mad.

<u>Paul:</u> No, I know you're not mad.

Not mad.

<u>Paul:</u> Not at all.

Not mad—I want do it—Zoup-zoon.

<u>Paul:</u> Mm, it's a lovely one. So shall we say cheerio and you can go with the lady. *(Mm.)*

Eileen said afterwards that this one was an *adult* with learning difficulties, rather than a child.

And to draw this chapter to a close, *(2013/07/08)* a dear old *asthmatic* gentleman:

I want my puffa! *(Some confusion at first as to what this meant)*

<u>Sarah:</u> Do you suffer from asthma? You can't breathe very well? *(Yes.)*

<u>Lilian:</u> Ah, okay, we'll get you some help—you won't need your *'puffa'*—in fact, it'll go away for good. *(Pause)* Okay, how are you feeling? It feels a bit easier, doesn't it? *(Yes)* Good—do you know where you are, or why you're talking to me? *(No.)* You felt pretty unwell, didn't you? *(Yes)* You really had a bad turn, with the breathing? *(Yes)* Did you wonder what would happen when you die—where you would go, or did you think that would be the end?

Yes, I was frightened.

<u>Lilian:</u> Well, you don't need to be frightened, because you're feeling fine, aren't you? You're not so uncomfortable.

Where am I?

<u>Lilian:</u> Well, you're just talking to me at the moment and then I'll explain what you have to do, we'll say, to get to 'Heaven', that's where you're going. You've finished with that body, which was rather worn out,

and you take on a brand-new body and you live in what I would call the Spirit world.

I'm not feeling comfortable.

Lilian: Not feeling comfortable? *(No)* Well, hold my hand and feel the strength coming through, and that should help you. *(Pause)* Tell me when you begin to feel…

Yes—feels stronger.

Lilian: Good—how old are you? *(92.)*

George: A good age!

My name's Jim.

Lilian: Hello Jim, mine's Lilian.

Lilian—you're marvellous.

Lilian: Try to be. *(Chuckle)*

You are marvellous.

Lilian: You just needed a little bit of help to go on into the Spirit world. *(Absolutely marvellous!)* Do you have a wife? *(No)* But a mum and a dad—we've all got a mum and a dad.

I had a wife, but she went twenty years ago.

Lilian: Well, there you are, you can go and have a meeting now—you'll see her. *(Will I?)* Yeah, is that what you want to do? *(Yes)* You can see your wife and your parents—any pets you might have had—a special dog?

Nobody's told me this before.

Lilian: No—a lot of people don't know. *(You're sure?)* Absolutely! So will you be in a minute, because you'll see a light ahead of you and within the light, you'll see someone waiting. *(Pause)*

Ooh—my goodness me! So there is! Yeah! So there is! Greta!

Lilian: You're going **Home**, you see.

I'm going home, I'm going Home! You're marvellous!

Lilian: I think what you need is to have a nice rest, don't you?

Yes, I'm very tired.

Lilian: Yes, and when you've had a rest, you'll feel completely well again—fit for anything!

Fit for anything…fit for nothing! *(Chuckles)*

Lilian: You'll be surprised. Happy to go?

Yeah—but you ARE MARVELLOUS!

Lilian: Well, thank you for that—to us, it's just a job, but we really are happy to do it.

You come and visit me?

Lilian: Well, I shall be here before too long, I'm in my eighties, so I won't be that long behind you.

Oh, don't tell my Greta that, she might not understand. *(Chuckles)* No, well my husband hopefully will be waiting for me.

Oh—I'm going, I can feel myself being pulled—it's rather nice!

Lilian: Good—we'll say bye-bye and know that you'll be okay.

Bye-bye lady, yes—I'll remember you—I'm going to call you 'blooming marvellous!

Lilian is BLOOMING MARVELLOUS! She recently got her *golden ticket HOME,* with so much Love. **xx**

Chapter 10

Golden Oldies

*I*f you look around, you will find the people who never need to use spectacles, who never have deficient hearing—all of their senses are intact. I have said to you, *find* those senses once again, it is never too late. Because you have allowed all of your senses to be depleted, what happens is that gradually they become more and more useless. That is why I have said to you, develop those senses; taste, smell, hearing, eyes—all that you have been endowed with, and there would be no reason for these things, these glasses, your hearing aids, your loss of smell and taste—all these things need not be.

Salumet 1994/11/21

This lady *(2022/02/14)* chose an *idyllic place* to make the *journey:*

Hello dear.

<u>Paul:</u> Hello and welcome to you.

It's got quite dark, yes. Are you waiting too?

<u>Paul:</u> Well, I was just waiting here, in case someone came. When you say, *'it's dark',* what were you doing before it got dark?

I'm waiting for my friend Peggy and I'm sitting on the river bank and it's very beautiful.

Paul: That sounds like a lovely idyllic spot.

Yes, and I think perhaps I've fallen asleep for a little while.

Paul: Do you know what happens…you've been brought here, because funnily enough, you're not at the river now.

Yes, I'm waiting for Peggy.

Paul: Well, actually you've been brought into this place—have you ever thought about what happens— do you believe in Heaven, or whatever happens when you die?

Oh yes, my dear, all the time! But, it's too beautiful a day to be thinking like that.

Paul: Well, it *is* a beautiful day. You've been brought here because something must have—I'm guessing that you were at an age where it could happen, and it sounds like you chose a beautiful, idyllic place, to fall asleep and pass on. And of course, you don't feel different, because there is no 'death.' So, it is a gentle moving on to what we call Spirit, or Heaven/Spirit realm.

Oh, it can't be that my dear, I felt someone touch my arm.

Paul: Ah, you felt a touch? *(Yes)* Well, that person that touched your arm, it could actually be someone known to you, who's already passed on—maybe a parent, friend, or grandparent?

I don't have too many relatives left.

Paul: Not on the Earth as such, but ones that have already passed? If you look forward, you may see a light, and I think you may recognise someone.

Yes, but I don't wish to leave this beautiful place, it's very beautiful.

Paul: All I say is, where you're going will be vastly and amazingly more beautiful, even than this bench by the river. Everybody says who goes to Heaven, which is where you'll be going, that's where we all go, you cannot even describe the beauty.

I'm sure it is very beautiful, but I'm not ready.

Paul: Not ready?

No, I want to stay here a while.

Paul: Well, you've been brought here because I think you *are* ready, you *are* ready.

Are you telling me I must go?

Paul: Well, I suppose it is *your* choice.

Oh, listen my dear, listen to the birds sing! Can you hear them? They're singing and singing!

Paul: Well, yeah, they may not be the river birds any longer, they may actually be the other birds, because they wouldn't be singing like that at night, I don't think.

(Sometimes music, birdsong or familiar voices are heard, gently relaxing/soothing/encouraging those in need)

If I go my dear, will you inform my friend Peggy? She'll be waiting for me.

Paul: Yes, Peggy will be told for sure, you don't need to worry about Peggy now, she'll understand, and she will be told. *(Well...)* So, you look forward now and you'll have a wonderful surprise—do you see a light?

I'm seeing a shape—it's almost like a tunnel, but it's full of light, yes.

Paul: Full of light and maybe those beautiful bird sounds were actually coming from that light?

Oh, it very well could be, yes okay, but if I go, can I come back?

Paul: Well, there are so many options... We're all allowed to come back and have other lives, yes, and there's ways of coming back, other ways of visiting, but for whatever reason, your *physical* body has 'died', but you still have your body—I can't explain it very well, but your body still exists, but it's not quite the same as your physical body, but it's actually *better. (The Etheric body)*

Do you know dear, there's an old lady down my street that's been telling me for ages that someone will meet me—is that true?

Paul: That's right, absolutely true, yes. You just have to look forward into the light, and I think those images will clarify for you, like clouds clearing, and you'll see someone, a face that perhaps you haven't seen for a long, long time.

Yes, please tell Peggy I'll be okay.

Paul: Yes, Peggy will be looked after.

I feel quite secure and happy. May I ask your name? (I'm Paul) *Paul on the bank of the river, okay.*

Paul: Lovely—yes.

Okay, I will go.

Paul: You'll be able to check in on Peggy and keep an eye on her, from where you're going.

Oh, I'll keep an eye on her, don't worry, she's my best friend. And your name was? (Paul) *Paul on the bank, thank you Paul.*

"No one suddenly changes when they come to our world. They still retain their freewill, they still retain *all* of their feelings, *all* of their prejudices; *all* remains the same. So, in our world, as in yours, some move on more quickly than others—It *all* depends on the Soul."

Salumet 1994/08/01

Next, *(2016/07/04)* an elderly gentleman on a *park bench*, preoccupied with *finding his dentures*:

I don't believe it! I can't believe it!

Sarah: What can't you believe?

I've lost my bleedin' teeth! (Chuckles)

Lilian: Perhaps we can help you.

Where the heck have they gone?

Lilian: Did somebody take them from you?

I don't know.

Lilian: Do you know where you are?

Where I am?—sitting in the bleedin' chair missus.

Lilian: Can you remember the room that you're in? Are you in a hospital? *(No!)* Your own home? You'll understand why I ask in a minute.

I'm on the park bench, aren't I—looking at the little birds.

Lilian: But you've lost your teeth; well, that's a shame.

I wonder if they're in them old sandwiches.

Lilian: I don't know.

Could you have a look for me dear?

Lilian: I will, I will, but if you'll just listen for a moment, it may help you. Did you feel unwell? *(No!)* No pain, no nothing? Never mind about your teeth for the moment.

Why? I got to—I can't afford another set.

Lilian: No—well, we'll find them, but did you have any pain—or just tired? Were you very tired?

I'm always tired my dear—always tired.

Lilian: So how old are you? *(92)* Oh, my word, that's a good age, isn't it? And you're sat in the park?

Sat in the park on the bench, watching them pretty little birds.

Lilian: I see, but did you ever think what would happen when you die, when your time was up and you died?

Yeah, of course I do, all the time.

Lilian: Did you think that was the end of it?

End of what?

Lilian: We'll say Heaven—did you ever think of going to Heaven?

I never thought I'd ever make there.

Lilian: Well, that's what's happened. Something has caused you to die.

What, and THIS is Heaven?

203

Lilian: You'll get there in a minute—you'll get there and your teeth—as long as you accept what I say.

How's my bleedin' teeth travel on their own?

Lilian: Well, you'd be surprised—anything can happen—but, you understand that you've died?

I find it a bit hard to believe it. If you find my teeth for me, I might...I ain't going to no bleedin Heaven without my teeth!

Lilian: Look in your hands and I think you might see your teeth.

Oh, good grief! Who put them there? Who put them in my hands?

Lilian: I think the person that's waiting to take you into Spirit put them there for you.

Well, you'll have to wait a minute. You wait a minute—I'll put them in. (Pause while hands go to put false teeth in mouth.) That feels better, doesn't it?

That's better!

Lilian: Yeah—I'm sure it does!

You got false teeth?

Lilian: I've got a few, so I know how it feels.

Oh right—bleedin' terrible—feel like you're slurping.

Lilian: I know! *(Chuckles)* Yes, but they are very necessary. But what I want you to do is to look ahead of you and you'll see a light and eventually in that light you'll see someone you'll probably know that's already 'died', and they'll be there to help you. So, tell me when...

I wonder if my Clara will come and meet me?

Lilian: Possibly, if that's what you want, that's probably what it will be.

I doubt it though.

Lilian: Well, first of all, you see the light—lovely bright light.

I don't know if I wanna go now.

Lilian: Well, I think it'll be best. *(Do you?)* Mm—it's where we *all* go; we start a new life in Spirit.

There's one thing I don't understand Miss. Isn't it bleedin' crowded?

Lilian: No—I think that's what most people think. No, I don't think it'll be too crowded. Somebody will be waiting there for you. *(You sure?)* Absolutely and I've got a feeling it's someone you really want to see.

Yeah—I suppose I better get into the habit of arguing with my Clara.

Lilian: It'll be nice to see her though, wouldn't it? *(Yeah.)* Tell me when you begin to...

I feel quite tired.

Lilian: Yes, you need a rest really, but let's get you, say, with Clara.

I see a small light. That's nice, I can hear a voice— Clara. Oh my God, she's not changed one bit!

Lilian: She can help you. Ready to go? *(I am.)* Yeah—when you've had a rest, you can start living again—only in Spirit.

Thank you my dear.

Lilian: Yeah, I'll let you go—I know you'll be fine.

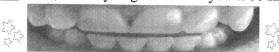

This next rescue, *(2023/03/06)* involves a gentleman using the expression, *'popped my clogs',* which is a colloquial way of describing *death*. Sabine, *(the medium)* whose first language is *French*, wasn't familiar with the expression:

Can I have a bit more coffee please? Just a little bit...

Paul: Well, can I just ask you...

Don't tell him—just give me a little bit, just a little bit please...

Paul: Well, I'm sure we can get you some—you've been feeling a bit unwell though, haven't you lately?

I know.

Paul: But you're feeling calmer now and better, aren't you?

(He continued to ask for more coffee.)

Paul: Yes, we'll get you a cup—it's coming.

Thank you!

Paul: How are you feeling in yourself now?

Better now I know that coffee is on the way.

Paul: Good—you were getting to that sort of age, weren't you? Had you thought much about what happens when we die?

Whoa—you just go on, don't you?

Paul: That's right! We *do* go on and people shouldn't be scared, because it's a lovely, beautiful thing and you get to reunite with all those that have gone before.

Ooh, really?

Paul: Yes, you do...

I never thought about that—Margaret never agreed to that...

Paul: Well, something must have caused you to—
sometimes we don't even realise when we have died.

Popped the clogs!

Paul: Yes, sometimes we don't even realise when it
happens to us—that's actually what's happened to
you.

Wow! I managed to do it!

Paul: You've done it! And what you should sense, is
a beautiful light.

Yeah, but I can't go without my coffee!

Paul: You can take your coffee with you, that's
fine...

I've popped my clogs then?

Paul: You have *popped your clogs,* and you'll find
you'll have beautiful coffees and much more
actually—it'll be a new start for you. Did you have a
loved one who's already passed?

**My Margaret's already there, but she says there's
nothing, but I don't believe her really.**

Paul: That's right, well you look ahead of you—can
you see a light?

**Well, I thought I might spring on her, make her
JUMP!**

Paul: Okay! If you're ready, do you see or sense a
beautiful light?

**Well, the thing is, if I come, she's gonna be there,
she's gonna see me first.**

Paul: Well, if you put the thought out there that you
don't want her to be there just yet...

You think I can go on my own?

Paul: You can put the thought out there that you want
it to be a *surprise...*

Yeah—oh, I know she'll love it!

Paul: Have a look then now for that light ahead of you. Got it?

Yeah, it's there all right.

Paul: Okay, and you're feeling good now, aren't you?

Much better now, yeah, my chest is free.

Paul: You may even see something in the light—I don't know what it could be…

I don't want it to be her!

Paul: It might just be someone with a cup of coffee.

Something else, not Margaret—I don't need a coffee anymore.

Paul: You just have a look into that light though—that's your doorway to heaven or whatever we want to call it. You may find yourself being pulled into it.

Yeah, this guy's gonna help me to surprise her, yeah.

Paul: Wonderful—do you feel yourself almost floating towards that light now?

Do you think I can ask him if he has another shirt for me?

Paul: Yes, you certainly can.

A clean shirt to go and see her…

Paul: I'm sure he'll sort that out for you—he'll be very happy to sort that out for you.

She'll jump—that'll be nice—alright, I'll go and place my order now, ay…

Paul: You go into that light now and have a lovely new life for yourself with Margaret and all the others.

Well, thank you and sorry I didn't drink your coffee.

<u>Paul:</u> That's fine—just happy that you're on your way now. Sometimes we just need a little point in the right direction.

Yeah, that's right sir, that's right sir—oh, wonderful!

"I would wish that your whole planet could move away from these occasions of *deep mourning*. When will you realise that death is not for sorrow, death is to *rejoice*, because to us my dear friends, it is your *birth*, it is your *birth* in returning '*HOME*' to those who have *loved* and who have *helped you* throughout your earthly trials."

Salumet 1997/09/01

This next rescue, *(2013/06/22)* involves an *upper-class* lady. In Spirit world the only '*riches*' that count are riches of *Spirit*:

<u>Lilian:</u> Good evening and welcome. *(Pause)*

Are you addressing me? (Yes.) ***Who allowed you entry? Who said you could come in here?***

<u>George:</u> Come in where? Where are you then, can you say?

I will have no men in this room! Will you please leave immediately!

(The lady only wished to speak with Lilian—though rescues are a team effort, sometimes it's better to have one speaker.)

<u>Lilian:</u> Yes, okay.

Now who are you?

Lilian: My name is Lilian.

Lilian? Lilian who?

Lilian: I am a friend who hopefully can help you.

No—Lilian who?

Lilian: Lilian Pearce, is that good enough?

Who said that you could enter this room?

Lilian: Well, I think *you've* entered into my friend's room.

I've entered in nowhere. Don't be so insolent!

Lilian: What were you sitting in before you came?

I was in a chair.

Lilian: What sort of chair?

(In exasperation) Why! Why! Why!

Lilian: If you bear with me, you'll understand. Were you sat in a *cane* chair?

—Of course not.

Lilian: Well, you feel the arms of the chair now, and you'll find you are sat in a *cane* chair.

(Feels chair arms)

Now who's playing tricks? Now you can see why I will not allow people into this room!

Lilian: It's not a trick. Have you ever thought what would happen when you died? Be quite honest about this.

Do you know? I am rather angry! I'm trying to contain myself.

Lilian: I do understand.

Why these questions?

Lilian: If you bear with me, you will understand.

Why should I bear with you?

Lilian: Did you feel ill or anything before I spoke to you?

210

Of course not.

Lilian: You didn't feel ill?

Of course not, I am sitting here.

Lilian: But you are not in your own room. There's something that has caused you to die, and you didn't accept what had happened, but what you do is you move on to the next world, the Spirit world.

I do not believe that! If I die, I will go to Heaven.

Lilian: Yes, you'll go to Heaven, but you haven't accepted it and that's why you're talking to me and that's why I am here to help you.

And who are you?

Lilian: I've just told you my name.

Lilian Pearce—but who ARE you?

Lilian: I'm just somebody who wishes to help people like you to understand what has happened to them. I've helped many people and they are really quite grateful in the end.

You really must go and fetch me a brandy, because my temper is near to boiling point!

Lilian: Well, first of all—

(Jan then asked Lilian to ask who the lady was.)

Lilian: Can you tell me who *you* are?

That matters not.

Lilian: Okay—do you feel very light in your body? *(Yes.)* And ahead of you, you can see a light? *(Mm.)* And people are there waiting to welcome you into Heaven—maybe someone that you know. I know I'm a stranger, and I'm sorry about that, but it just needs someone to tell you what has happened.

I am so annoyed, so annoyed. I understand, you are probably a very kind person…

Lilian: I'm trying to be, but like you, I could lose my temper and what good would that do?

I would have you removed immediately!

Lilian: Well, there you are—but I would like to help you.

I will listen because you are persevering, and I can feel my blood-pressure rise.

Lilian: Well, my job *is* to persevere.

What IS your job? Just to help?

Lilian: Just to help people like you to accept what has happened. We all have to die at some time, but there are people like you who just don't accept what has happened.

Are you implying I am difficult? Is that what you're saying?

Lilian: No, you are just not understanding at the moment.

No—I surely am not.

Lilian: I wish you were, but I would like you to look for the light.

And what will this light look like?

Lilian: A bright warm light, and in it you should begin to see people that you will recognise.

Not many I want to meet.

Lilian: There will be somebody there you will want to meet—I don't know who, but you will know them.
(Pause)

Well! If they think they'll tell me what to do, they can think again! How dare they! How VERY dare they! I can hear them.

Lilian: And you recognise them?

Yes, I do. Young upstarts! Okay.

Lilian: But you're fond of them.

I would never tell them that! Why would I tell them that?

Lilian: But they know that already. *(Do they?)* Yes—don't forget, you're going to Heaven, where things will be much clearer.

I'll have a few things to say when I get there. How long will it take?

Lilian: Well, you're there almost. *(Pause)*

Now that really is beautiful—that is wonderful! And if you are telling me the truth, then I am happy to go.

Lilian: I'm telling you the truth.

Jan: We are.

Who's that other voice?

Lilian: That's another lady who is here to help.

(Okay, okay.) I'm just glad you've accepted—that's all that's needed.

Who would have guessed that we would have needed a 'Lilian Pearce' to help ME into Heaven?

Lilian: Well, you never know...

But I am going and I thank you—good bye.

Lilian: You're very welcome.

Jan: Before you go, could you just tell us your name?

I certainly will not! You will not know me, so I will not tell you. So good bye—I have to go. They are pulling, pulling, pulling. And I of course am not a commoner.

Jan: I gathered that.

Well, that's enough information for now.

Lilian: Well, you've had a commoner to help you.

Well, I've become quite attached to you.

Lilian: Well, thank you—as long as you're okay. *You're still a little impudent, but there you go. I must go …*

Rescues can provide interesting *glimpses* into the *lives of others*, but the *important thing* is *simply* to get them *HOME*.

This next dear lady *(2006/01/03)* was 101 and also preoccupied with finding her teeth:
Can you fetch my teeth dearie?
Lilian: You need your teeth, do you?
Sarah: Where did you leave them? *(Who's that?)*
Lilian: You don't recognise the voices, do you? What do you remember, what have you been doing?
I've been having a little nap and I woke up and my teeth have gone.
Lilian: Well, you can have some nice new teeth.
I don't want any more bleedin' teeth—just fetch my own.
Lilian: I need to explain something to you, because you're quite an elderly person, aren't you?
You're as old as you feel, and I feel pretty old.
Lilian: Do you? How old are you? *(101.)* Are you really! That's a good age. Well, I have to tell you that while you were asleep, I think your heart stopped and caused you to die. So, where you belong now, is, I'll say, in *'Heaven'*—that word probably means more to you?

214

More likely to be a gate! No, not expecting to go there.

Lilian: That's where we *all* go.

Not without my teeth!

Lilian: You can take your teeth with you.

Where are they?

Lilian: Somebody will have them waiting for you. What you need to do, is to…

What do you mean, 'somebody will have them'?

Lilian: Well, just listen for a moment, you'll see a bright Light in front of you.

I can't see much dearie.

Lilian: You will, you will! You'll see a bright light, and in that light, you'll see someone that you'll recognise—someone that has died before you. *(Pause) (Well, well!)* Nice surprise?

It's my little Maisie! How did she get here?

Lilian: She's been waiting for you—you just needed someone to tell you what had happened.

Get my teeth quick, dearie! (Chuckles)

Lilian: Has she got your teeth?

I can't see her without my teeth in.

Lilian: You won't need false teeth, you'll have brand new ones, as you did when you were young.

Well, that's a bleedin' miracle.

Lilian: Well, there you go!

Yeah, that's my Maisie—Maisie!

Lilian: And you're happy to go with Maisie, are you? She'll help you.

I'm happy to see my Maisie. (Good) *Waited a long time for this. Why couldn't I see her before then?*

Lilian: Well, you just needed someone to tell you—that's all. *(Who are you anyway?)* Just someone who tells you where to go and what to look for. It's a job that we do.

It's made me quite tired. I think I'll have a little nap.

Lilian: You go with Maisie and you can have a rest and then you can recoup—and I think you'll have a lovely time. So, we'll say cheerio.

I'll come back and see you, dearie—when I've found my teeth.

Lilian: Yeah, lovely—we'll look forward to that!

Next, *(2019/02/11)* a gentleman who had been brought to other *rescue circles* previously, but remained *unconvinced*:

Paul: Hello, you are welcome to speak.

And who may you be?

Paul: My name's Paul.

You won't convince me.

Paul: Oh, right, what is it I'm supposed to try to convince you about?

You know, about following a light!

---

[10] Author's great grandmother, who went *Home* at 105 years!

216

<u>Paul</u>: Ah, that's right, yes.

I'm not having any of it.

<u>Paul</u>: Ah yes, so you know what's happened to you, do you?

No, of course I do and I don't believe a word!

<u>Paul</u>: Right, well, what's the last thing you do remember?

None of your business.

<u>Paul</u>: Ah, so you don't accept that you…

First of all, who are you?

<u>Paul</u>: Well, I'm Paul and I've been brought to you, to try to help you.

I've been through all this before, three other times!

<u>Paul</u>: Perhaps you needed to come here to have it explained to you—we'll try to talk it through with you again—it may suddenly make sense to you, that's all—I'll try to make it make sense for you.

Do you know what the last one said to me?

<u>Paul</u>: No, I don't.

That I was rather a silly man! Who does he think he is?

<u>Di</u>: That's not very kind.

No, you seem a little different.

<u>Paul</u>: Good—thank you, we try our best—we get others brought to us and we try to gently explain what has happened, and it's not anybody's fault, it's not really explained probably what happens when we 'die' and the fact is, there *is* such a place, a bit like Heaven or whatever you want to call it, when our bodies have finished—life goes on—It's fantastic…

Look, if you're going to keep talking, I would like a cup of coffee.

217

Paul: A cup of coffee? Well, I'm sure that can definitely be arranged. Just to check, are you feeling okay now?

I feel fine.

Paul: Good. So, we'll try to get that cup of coffee for you. Is there anyone at all that you've known who's passed already, because if you know anyone, it makes it easier—they can actually come and explain it to you, because they already know a lot more.

Well—this is such a nuisance...

Paul: It will begin to make sense—I can promise you that.

Who do I know that's gone where?

Paul: That's already passed on, passed away. Do you know a grandparent or someone that's already passed, or a parent?

Yeah, that's a silly question! Everybody's got grandparents!

Paul: Right, is there any one of them that you liked a bit more than others?

Yes. My little grandmother was really kind. Yes, she had lots of love for lots of people.

Paul: Well, I think, if you can see that little light.

Mm, I've tried this one before.

Paul: Have you tried before to look for your grandmother? *(No.)* Well let's have a little look again, if she's able to come to the light, if you can find her, she will explain everything to you a lot better than I can. *(Pause)*

Oh my God! She looks too young!

Paul: That's often said, that's right.

218

Is it really her? You're not kidding me my boy, are you?

<u>Paul</u>: Absolutely not, no. if you talk to her, you'll sense her, you'll know it's her, you'll *feel* it's right.

You know what, I feel I want to cry, I'm so happy.

<u>Paul</u>: Well, you've got lots to_look forward to now— you've made the big step, now all you have to do is to go with your grandmother, and I'm sure she'll have a beautiful cup of coffee for you, yes.

I am speechless...speechless...

<u>Paul</u>: You don't need to say anything, you're happy to go with her now?

Will you stay close by?

<u>Paul</u>: I will stay here, because I may have others to help from this end, but I am very happy that we were able to help *you,* and your grandmother will look after you well now.

I feel very, very light.

<u>Paul</u>: Yes, yeah, that's fine, it's good, you can leave all your troubles behind and go into the light and find out lots of new things.

Eileen said afterwards: *"I don't know how you did that Paul, he was stubborn—I hope his grandmother tells him off!"*

Eileen—much loved medium and full-trance channel for Salumet.

The final rescue of the chapter involves a member of the *clergy*. *God/The Great Creative Force* makes no distinction between *religions, with the knowledge that ALL are divine sparks from the One Source*. This man wished to be met by *Jesus*, so this is what he experienced. *(See 'The Light Escort' in Appendix 1 for information about how transitions are arranged.)* The rescue *(2019/03/11)* began with clairvoyance from Di, about a *white book* with a *gold cross:*

That's my book!

Di: Did you leave it somewhere?

Somebody stole it from me.

Di: I am really sorry to hear that. Were you in church? *(Yes.)* Can you remember who stole it from you?

I don't know who did, but I'm sure it was those nasty children. They keep on coming over here and rifling things about.

Di: I'm sorry that they're upsetting you.

They're little rascals. I wish I never had to deal with them.

Di: Do you teach them in church or something?

Yes, that's the task I've been appointed to.

Di: Like a Sunday school teacher?

Not only Sunday, it's everyday—starts at 6 o'clock in the morning and you better be there!

Jan: Are you a nun?

No, I am not a nun!

Jan: Sorry, you're a gentleman.

Yes, thank you very much…

Jan: So, you are a priest or you belong to an order?

Yes, I belong to an order. I am Brother Henry.

Jan: Brother Henry, nice to meet you. I'm sorry the children are giving you lots of problems, I'm sure they are just being mischievous, aren't they? They are just being children.

Well, who needs them anyway…

Jan: We all need children and don't forget you were a child once, I'm sure you did naughty things.

Well, that wasn't something very nice to go through.

Jan: Okay—anyway, what was the last thing that you remember, apart from losing your prayer book—was that the last thing that you remember?

Well, I was searching for it.

Jan: Right, well, the reason my friend picked up your book. *(Meaning 'picked up' psychically, rather than physically picking up the book)*

Yeah, well why doesn't she give it back?

Jan: Well, the reason why she found your book in the first place, is that you've been brought back to us to enable us to explain to you what's happened.

You are not making any sense.

Jan: Well, being a man of a cloth and being Roman Catholic, yes? *(Yes.)* I'm not quite sure what the Roman Catholic faith believe happens to us after death; could you explain that to me?

When we die, we go to Heaven when we've been good.

Jan: And you would obviously consider yourself to be a good man of the cloth, yes?

I get up every day and I teach those children, even if I don't want to, I do my part!

<u>Jan</u>: Right, what if I told you, Brother Henry, that actually you've gone to Heaven and that you're talking to me from Heaven.

It doesn't sound like Heaven at all at the moment!

<u>Jan</u>: You in fact have died, and I think whatever caused you do die—you're kind of in the middle at the moment—you haven't quite got to Heaven yet—not that you're not going there, don't get me wrong, you're kind of in 'limbo'. So, we need to try and get you to the next stage. Had you been poorly? *(No.)* Right, did you have any pain? Do you remember any pain in your chest?

Yes, I had a pain in my chest earlier.

<u>Jan</u>: You did, yeah, well I'm sorry to tell you, Brother Henry, I think that you had a heart-attack and you died. Okay? I know that's rather a huge shock and you may think that I'm rather silly, but that's what's happened to you.

Well, I don't quite feel 'dead'!

<u>Jan</u>: Well, no, because when we pass over to Spirit, we still feel the same. We still pass over as ourselves and you will find it very strange, but I can assure you that's what's happened to you.

So, what's next? Do I have to see those children again?

<u>Jan</u>: No, no you don't have to teach the children again, you don't need to see the children again if you don't want to.

Well, that's excellent news—do you have any other nice ones?

<u>Jan</u>: Again, I don't know what your belief was, would you imagine that Mary would meet you?

No, I think Jesus would come and collect me.

<u>Jan</u>: Jesus will collect you, okay. Now obviously Jesus is a divine light, yes? Would you agree?

Yes, he is.

<u>Jan</u>: So, if you close your eyes, and think of Jesus, in a way that you've always thought of Jesus, he's going to appear to you as a bright light.

HHHHOOOOOO!

<u>Jan</u>: So, I now want you to walk into that light and be with Jesus, and it's what we call, the *Spirit world*, which is where Jesus is, in the *Spirit world*.

HHHHOOOOO he's so magnificent!

<u>Jan:</u> It's the light that emanates from Heaven.

I've never seen a light like that before.

<u>Jan</u>: Yeah, you need to follow, go towards that light and other people on the other side will explain to you everything that you need to know.

HHHOOOOOO ooh WOW!

<u>Jan</u>: Okay? Can you do that for me?

Are you sure I can?

<u>Jan</u>: Of course, yes you can. Just go.

(Whispering) ***Do you think he will let me in?***

<u>Jan</u>: Of course, Spirit world let *everybody* in—it's where we *all go*, it's where we *all belong*. You need to go—we're all *God's children*, we're all the same; it's where we *all* go. I want you to follow that light and all will be explained to you. Okay? ***(Okay.)***

"I am unhappy sometimes to hear that this word *'religion'* is still so important in your world. It would be much better to use the, *'Love of Mankind,'* that he could bond together from every area of society, to make a *Unified Religion*—I say reservedly, the 'religion' of *Love and of Brotherhood*. I know that your world religions have served the people well—If it has caused them to have comfort, so be it; but *NOW* is the time to place it all to one side and everyone to *join together*, to seek for that God-consciousness, which is within you all—but it is coming…"

Salumet 1994/11/07

To wrap things up, let's **dive** with *Salumet*, into how to *send* healing *thoughts/prayers more effectively*:

Serena: *How* is the best way to send them and what should we really do to get the maximum effect?
Your thoughts must be made in Love and dedication to the knowledge that it is being received by those of us in Spirit who wish to help with the healing. I would say 'Love' is the utmost thing to have when you are sending thoughts for another.
You must remember also my dear friends that it is not permissible to interfere with another's life once you have come to the Earth plane. But yes of course, loving thoughts are always dealt with; but you do not always have the results that you want. When we receive healing thoughts, whatever is best for that person will be fulfilled, and that is not always what you would wish for; you have to understand—you understand, don't you? *(Agreed)*

When things are difficult for any one of you, do not immediately say: why me? Because, why *not* you? There is a whole world of people, and most I would say have encountered problems and troubles at some stage of their lives. We in Spirit are here to help, I have told you often that you must ask for that help before we can give out the help that is needed.

Let us for example take: if everyone is praying for someone who is ill, and you have interfered with the passing of that loved one. That is not what you would desire, would you? *(Agreed)* No—so therefore it is best to give the loving thought and allow us in Spirit to deal with it. And I wish to say one more thing about this, that it takes only one loving thought, if it is genuine and sent with Love, for it to be dealt with. There is no need for the repetition of thought. (Ah!) You seem surprised my dear friend—

Lilian: Yes, sometimes you feel a little bit desperate…

Then what would happen is that those who are dealing with loving thoughts would try to help you also, because you have difficulty with accepting what is to be.

Paul: Part of sending prayers is that you're sending *Love*, which is an *energy* and some illnesses might take several *'sendings'* to help?

If you have sent one genuine loving thought, it is received. If you continue to ask for help over and over and over, do you not see that you have created a doubt?

225

<u>Paul:</u> I see yes—you've mentioned that before, **(Yes)** about not asking for '*help*' as such **(Yes)** but just sending *Love…*

And to trust in that Great Creative Force that they know what is best for that person. Yes, but we understand that you are human, but if you are to be doing it day and night and on and on, it is wasted energy.

<u>Paul:</u> I can see that that could show your own inner doubt. **(Yes)**

<u>Sarah:</u> I remember you saying that repetition just becomes something you're *saying*—you're not getting that same in-depth feeling….

Yes—it is a little like the religions of your world who are constantly repeating the same words and after a while those words become a little meaningless.

<u>George:</u> I guess the repetitive prayer is more for praying for planetary conditions and large groups who seem to require more awareness?

No! Again, one prayer, if it is honest and loving and truthful should be enough. What would help is if you have a *group* of people sending that Love energy to us—that is helpful.

<u>Sarah:</u> So, what we do at meetings, asking for help— that's our energies going into that one thought?

Yes, but also not to be disappointed. So often you human beings are disappointed when your thoughts are not used in the way that you think. Yes, so trust—trust in the Great Creator that things *will* be utilised for the better.

<u>Paul:</u> What happens with the thought when we just send Love to wherever it's most needed?

Yes, it will be used to help the person named and then it will become part of the energy field.

<u>Paul:</u> Right—so if I don't name a person…

—If you can *feel* the person. If you do not know the name—If you can feel that person's energy then that is acceptable.

<u>Paul:</u> What if it's just a general thought to all humanity?

Then we in spirit will use that thought—yes, it is all to be used. I have told you previously that energy can be transmuted. You have to remember all of these teachings to fully understand.

<u>Paul:</u> Yes, so presumably if it's a general thought for all humanity…

Yes, a loving thought—and this is the important word—the 'Love' behind the thought will never be wasted or changed to be meaningless.

Salumet 2016/01/18

Chapter 11

Waves of Grieving Energy

*W*hy should you feel pity and sorrow for a Soul who is returning *HOME?* Should not instead you be giving thanks to that Great Creative Force for returning that Soul from whence it came? Until you take control of your *thinking*, of your own *emotional body*, there will always be stress, there will always be distress, there will always be hurt within your hearts and, after all, as I have said, why should you grieve for the Soul who is returning *HOME?*

Salumet 1999/07/05

The main aim of this chapter is to understand and *bring comfort* to those who are grieving. This young girl's *heartfelt words* speak volumes: *(2023/04/03)* Sabine was *'seeing'* a *red ball*, and then *Amanda* was speaking through Eileen:

I can get a red ball if you like?

Sabine: That would be nice.

Can you help my daddy?

Paul: Can we help your daddy? Possibly, yeah, I'm sure we can. How does your daddy need some help then?

He doesn't believe I'm in a lovely place. 'Cos I'm 'dead', you know?

<u>Paul:</u> Ah yes, we know all about that and it *is* a lovely place, you're absolutely right!

But daddy won't listen, he just keeps crying all the time.

<u>Paul:</u> Yeah, people grieve without understanding that their loved ones are in a beautiful, lovely place.

Yeah—he used to tell me that mummy was with the flowers—she had lovely flowers, but not in the ground. What can I do?

<u>Paul:</u> Well, have they told you, you can maybe visit him in his dream-state?

Yes, but he just keeps crying and won't listen.

<u>Paul:</u> Mm, maybe he can be influenced...

He didn't expect me to die before him—now he's left all on his own.

<u>Paul:</u> Yeah—if he could be nudged to go to a medium or a spiritualist church or something...

Mummy keeps showing herself to him and he still won't believe it and now I feel like I'm getting upset.

<u>Paul:</u> Yeah, I don't know if we could help in any way—we could send *Love* to him—if you were to tell us your daddy's name? *(Peter.)* Do you have his surname as well, but you could direct it—I'm sure it'll get *'posted'* to the right address, because you're here.

I used to tell daddy that I saw the Angels as well—I think he thinks I'm a bit strange.

<u>Paul:</u> Yeah, a lot of people, *until* they go to Heaven *themselves*, they *doubt it* all the way. The grieving *does* get *better* though. How long—I suppose you

don't know how much *'time'*, because it's different now, but all we can say is, *it DOES GET BETTER!*

I was listening when you were all asking for people. Can you do that for my daddy?

Paul: Yes, we'll do that for your daddy. What's your name? *(Amanda.)* Okay, so for Amanda's daddy. *(Peter)* Peter—that's right…

Are you dead as well?

Paul: No, not yet no, we're not.

So why have you got light?

Paul: Well, we meet every week at this time, because we've got these wonderful mediums, like the one you're using, so we can talk to you in Heaven, even though we're not *'dead'*, we're on Earth still.

I think it's wonderful.

Paul: It *is* wonderful! We don't really know how it works to be honest, but it *does* work and I know the *Power of Thought* and *Love,* work as well.

I think I should be the grown up and smack his bottom! (Laughter) He needs to listen to mummy. (Agreed) You're all very nice people.

Mark/Sara: Thank you! You're very nice too!

Paul: He'll get there in the end and he'll get the message at some point.

Yes, and I think you'll be nice to him.

Eve: We'll send him our Love.

Paul: That's right, we'll send him so much Love…

He might listen to someone else and not just mummy and me.

Mark: If we bump into someone called Peter…

Are you 'dead'?

Mark: No, I'm not 'dead' either, not yet.

<u>Paul</u>: No, we're not dead yet, but we can help a little bit with our *Thoughts.*

Yes—don't worry about it.

<u>Paul</u>: No, because everything works out in the end.

<u>Eve</u>: And don't *you* worry about it either.

I know, but I feel daddy needs some help. He's living there nicely, but because he can't see mummy, he's just distressed.

<u>Mark</u>: Well, you've done everything you can do, within your power.

<u>Sara</u>: You've done very well, to come here and ask for help.

Yes. Can I ask what your name's are? (We introduced ourselves)

Mummy's saying to this Paul, get up off your knees, it can be bad. (Paul had been kneeling next to Eileen, who was channelling Amanda.)

<u>Paul</u>: That's right, I *did* start aching a bit, so I'm sitting on the chair now—good advice, *'Hello',* tell your mum, *'Thank you'*—yeah.

She was quite strict sometimes.

<u>Paul</u>: But she's lightened up a bit now, I'm sure.

Yes, she's lovely. She thought daddy would speak to me now, but he's not been doing that.

<u>Sara</u>: He'll feel a bit happier in a while and then he'll be able to listen, I expect.

<u>Paul</u>: Yeah, it's all a bit of a shock at first, but it gets better with time.

Someone called 'Cho' said I've got to come now.

<u>Paul</u>: Ah yeah, Cho's our friend. But it's been lovely talking Amanda, thank you for *coming* and if we can help in any way, we certainly will try to.

231

Maybe I could bring lots of people to you?
<u>All:</u> Yeah! *(Chuckles)*

Oh dear, Cho's saying, 'no you won't'! *(Chuckles)*
Cho is a wonderful *cheeky Spirit friend* and *'gatekeeper',* overseeing who comes through the trance-mediums and helping to *protect* the circle. We included Amanda's dad in our prayers. Our modern busy lifestyles can make it harder to *'see'* and *'hear'* the *whispers of Spirit*, but there are so many wonderful stories of how nature and the animals, birds, insects, and many things, convey *loving messages*—we just need to be *open* and *relaxed* about sharing our thoughts/fears/doubts—**sharing** can be *powerful medicine.* Good *Psychics, Clairvoyants, Sensitives, Spiritualist churches* and others can help *reassure* people that *loved-ones* are *safe* and *happy. Psychic work* is not easy and sometimes conditions are not *right.* Of course, there are a few *'bad'* ones around, but that's the case in all *work*, whether it's *car salesmen, cowboy builders, world leaders…*

<u>*Let's **dive** with Salumet into the grieving process:*</u>
"I would like just to say to also remember those who are left behind on your Earth-plane—they *truly* are the ones who *suffer.* Those who come to our world quickly recognise what a beautiful and wonderful situation they have found themselves in; they have returned to knowledge and to all of those who Love them so. But they are also drawn back to this Earth-plane, to those who are suffering at their

232

loss—no matter how many times you tell them that their loved ones are safe and well, still so many mourn and mourn for much *too long*. So, therefore it is imperative that you, my dear friends, remember to ask for them also in your prayers. If only you could hear the cries of those left behind, you would understand how much and how much more that they are the ones to suffer. And yet it is a mourning which is unnecessary, because I can reassure you, each one of you, that when you return *HOME*, there is so much *Light*, so much *Love*, so much *happiness*.

You see, my dear friends, I say sad times only exist on this Earth, not in our world. It is a rejoicing that keeps us in our world—rejoicing that another Soul has departed the body and returned to the place that is much more *real* for them. But of course, any help that can be given to any human being, not only at a time of loss, but at all stages of earthly life—that can only be good—yes.

<u>Sara:</u> We can try to increase their awareness perhaps? You may try to do this. It may not always be accepted, but—yes, to speak easily about death and passing can only bring more knowledge to your world. We know that you all do this in different ways—a touch, a smile, a word—it takes very little to uplift the Soul—yes.

<u>Lilian:</u> I was just thinking, I bet in most cases where people are grieving on the Earth, there are strange coincidences which should give an *inkling* that everyone is okay?

Yes, there will always be an opportunity given to those who are left behind, in order that they may begin to think '*why*'. But then, of course as you know, it is entirely up to them, whether they accept or deny. You cannot do more than to offer your Love and your sympathy. But if you imagine how many have passed to Spirit on this one day alone, then you will have some idea of those who are in a state of grief."

Salumet 2015/02/23

Next, Salumet (1997/09/01) comments on the passing
of Princess Diana and the effects of mass-mourning:

Princess Diana was affectionately known as *The People's Princess'*. She expressed great *sympathy* for those in need, speaking out against the *atrocities of war* and controversial issues that others in her position usually evade, earning her a *special place* in our hearts.

Les: I was thinking about all the good work she has done and the tremendous emotional response—most extraordinary. I come to the question about leaving according to a *'prearranged plan'*, or leaving this life *earlier*, via *freewill*, on the part of another. Are there ever *any circumstances*, in which your world would be permitted to interfere with freewill?

We *know* and *feel* of the great *emotional Love*, which has arisen from your planet. I will say only this to you my dear friend: The endeavour to work well in your world, does not give you a passport to eternity. We know and we understand that when someone who has touched the hearts of many, passes to our world, it leaves you all feeling at a loss. But let me say this to you: Freewill cannot be interfered with whilst you remain on this earthly planet; there is no circumstance which would allow us to make that interference—it will not happen. You know and you understand that when you come to this life, you know *when* you will return to us. We can help, we can support, we can encourage, but we cannot *interfere,* we cannot interfere with freewill. I do not feel that you can truly understand the Great Plan that lies before. When you see a young woman such as you speak of, you see her only in her physical clothing, who has done 'good' in your world. Let me say this to you: Rejoice my friends, for she has returned *Home,* as have the others who were with her. It is not for any one of you to consider these happenings as what you term *'tragedies'*—they are not, they are part of the *Plan of Living* in your world. I can tell you that this lady, who has become known to you all, had a premonition of her life's end, but because of the *pace of living,* she would never have spoken openly about it. She was indeed a spiritual being, who had grown much over the last few years of her living. This may not be known to you, but her spiritual knowledge was quite great. And therefore, that is why the humanitarian side of her nature came to the fore, as she grew older in your earthly years.

I would like to say to you all, she has become an idol in your world. You feel sad at her passing, because of young years, because of the goodness that could be seen. I say this to you my dear friends: Look not to any idol in your world, because in doing so, you diminish the expression of Love that belongs, or *should* belong to *all* of mankind. I know you may find my words to be harsh, they do not mean to sound so, but I wish you all to look beyond your physical thinking once more. Always we must return to the spiritual being and what lies ahead.

Rejoice for her, for the life that she has led. Although she has endured many troubles as most of you do. After all, how can you grow if you do not face adversity? She is special only to you, because of her position in life—she has achieved no more than many unknown people who are exercising their Love of humanity around your planet. *(Agreed)* So, in realising this, dear friends, send out joy for the life that she led, for the Love she bestowed on others and look forward to knowing that she will continue in giving Love to those she has left behind.

She was with us quickly, if that will ease your burden of mind. I would wish that your whole planet could move away from these occasions of *deep mourning.* When will you realise that death is *not* for sorrow, death is to *rejoice,* because to us my dear friends, it is *your birth*, it is your birth in returning *HOME* to those who have *loved* and who have *helped* you throughout your earthly trials.

Les: That has given us great comfort and we do appreciate you telling us, particularly that it wasn't an act of *freewill* of others.

236

Her time was here—her time had come. Do not mourn her, she will know that she has been much-loved—she is aware! I do not wish you to speak of anyone who passes to this world, as if they are forgotten—they are *vibrant*, they are *alive*, more *alive* than you my dear friends. So, mourn not, but rejoice in the life that she has lived.

Les: Thank you very much for that—we do hope that in time this whole planet will be aware that they should not mourn, but be joyful when death occurs. I would like to say only this to you: If only you could feel the vibrations of grief that exudes from your world, when occasions such as we speak of occur, you would be shocked by them. The whole energy pattern which surrounds your planet is affected by such grief. It affects not only the vibrations of your Earth, but those who await those who come to us. It is difficult to surround the planet with Love, when so much grief abounds. That is why I ask you dear friends, in your individual thoughts, hopes and desires, that you replace *grief* with *Love*, with loving thoughts for all those who are in need.

~Transformed (not lost!) and not forgotten.~

Of course, there are times when tears flow and that's beautiful. With understanding, tears will transform more easily into *tears of joy,* because though we miss the *physical presence deeply,* we take great comfort in the knowledge that they are ***HOME*** and we can still *feel, hear* and sometimes even *smell* them— speaking from personal experience!

"Sadness and happiness are part of the *same bubble.* So, it is good when we hear *laughter* and *tears* together—it means that progress is being made by those left behind."

Salumet 2023/09/11

Chapter 12

Beyond the Tunnel of Light
~Returning *HOME*~

Y ou know that when you leave these *physical bodies*, when you come to *our side of life*, you will gravitate to that plane of existence which is suited to you *spiritually*. It will belong to the vibration from which you come that you will go to.

Salumet 2001/02/19

So far we have focussed on the *transition to Spirit world*. In this chapter, we'll dive into the *architecture* of our *true HOME*. In Spirit world *THOUGHTS* are of *supreme importance*. The *purity* of our loving-thoughts helps *shape* our experience, both *here* and *HOME*, which is why Salumet's *central teaching* is the *Power of Thought:* Learning control/mastery of *Thought will* help the earthly experience as well as when returning *HOME*, which is like a *Land of THOUGHT ENERGY:*

Jesus answered him, **"Truly I tell you, today you will be with me in paradise"** *Luke 23:43 NIV*

So, let's **dive** with *Salumet* into this *paradise* that *Jesus* was *harping on* about: ♫ ♪

Les: We had a charming little girl through, *(from Spirit world)* who described how the flowers *spoke and sang* to her and how the *water changes colour* and other very *beautiful comments*. She, I imagine could not understand having to *THINK* those things, so am I right in presuming that they exist for her to see and anybody else?

There are areas in our world, which are open to all. As you would expect in your world, to go to water, to go to mountains, to go to fields, wherever—so too can this happen in our world. It is open to all who wish to seek. You understand?

Les: Yes, so our thoughts would be *'homing into'* the Creator's thoughts, which had already produced that scene?

The thought always exists, let me put it that way. You will travel along the *Energy of Thought,* when you are capable of doing so. Again, it is a matter of how much you have learned.

All of you who come to our side of life, arrive at where you *belong*, to where you have '*earned*'. It matters not, whether you say what they know on this Earth, as far as Spirit matters go, you dear friend, cannot know what they have achieved. You cannot *judge* and say, this one/that one does not deserve this, because only they and the *Great Creator*, knows what has happened in this lifetime.

240

<u>Les:</u> I wouldn't presume to judge, but I'd want to know that I'm doing the right thing with rescues, telling them it is a ***happy place.***

Of course: Most of you upon this earthly plane, will have no problems at all, when you return *HOME*—**even those of you who think they do not know much. But that is not what is important, it is what they have *done*, what they have *achieved* within their lifetimes here. Because they do not speak about what you term *'spiritual matters'*, does not mean they are not *spiritual.*

Salumet 1996/07/29

 <u>*Who decides where we go / life review?*</u>

<u>Sallie:</u> Talking about *levels of darkness*, are they self-imposed?

Of course—yes, you are the judge. Your actions in this world will determine your placement in the Spirit realms. Of course, no-one places you in places of *'darkness'*—that is what you have sought for yourselves; it is self-inflicted, but many of the teachings that have been given to you human beings over many aeons of time, have described these places of what you term *'darkness,'* not very well. They have been termed—shall we take an example of your Christian teaching, being called *'hell.'* Yes, I think you are familiar with this term, and of course, there is no *burning fire* as that religion would teach you, but of course, there is the 'hell' of your *own* doing. But you are fully responsible for all places that you find yourself— but you are never left alone.

Sara: Even if by the time we leave Earth, we have evolved much *spiritually*, do we *still* have to *relive every moment* of *'ignorance'*—do we relive *everything,* when we come over?

Yes, all is made clear to you—

Sara: What a *shame! (Chuckles)*

Yes, you cannot just see the good moments.

Sara: I don't mean just the good, but I wonder if *everything*?

Every second of your existence will be shown to you. (Oh!) Many things that would, at this time, seem very insignificant to you, all of these things become magnified. But do not despair, because most souls return to our world and realize how much good that they have done. When we speak of darker realms, I want you to know that it is the minority. Don't be afraid—do not place upon yourselves fear or guilt—we do not wish you to do that. Most human beings have more '*good*' than '*wrong*' within them. And after all, it is the gestures that you are unaware of, which spiritually are the greatest. You seem surprised?

Sara: So, it isn't always a painful experience to relive the earthly life?

I would not say painful, but to most I would say there are some surprises. (I'm sure!) Yes, but all of this happens very quickly and quite soon after you come to our world.

Lilian: So, if there's something we're really, really, sorry about at that particular time, we can put it right, can we?

Of course, the opportunity—can I say this to you, that the *recognition* is the greatest part of the '*putting right*'. In recognizing that your actions or your words are wrong, you have gone most of the way in correcting. But can I just say this to you, that if you *know* you have done something—and you *do* know, you intuitively know when you have—and I would say this to you before I continue, that the worst thing you can do is to hurt another human being, not only with actions, but with words and above *all* with your *thoughts.* I would say this to you, my dear friends—and this is important for you to know: If you can put right a wrong, then do so while you are upon this planet. And, I will repeat myself: it *can* be done with the power of your *Thought.* It is much better for the soul if you do that whilst in the human form.

Salumet 1999/11/15

What about people with specific beliefs?

Ben: I recently lost a relative and they were a '*Jehovah Witness*'. I wonder if you'd comment on how they are getting on in *Spirit world*?

"Yes—I will say this to you: that there are so many religions within your world, no matter what title you choose to follow, whether it be the *Christianity* or any other—all peoples are destined for the *same place*—with that, I mean the *World of Spirit.* Your dear relative, if they were happy to be, as you call them, '*Jehovah's Witnesses*', was *happy* with that life, was *happy* that they had a *good life*, that they harmed no-one, nor pressed another to take

243

their point of view, then they will of course come directly to Spirit. But what happens sometimes, is that when they are so set in their ways, or have such *strong beliefs*, that they are drawn to the same kind of people. You may not realise that this can happen and that everyone intermingles, no matter who or what they are. If their religion was so strong that they would still retain it for a while, then your relative will be with those like-minded people, and what eventually happens is that they begin to recognise that there is no need for religious names—that each one is in the image of the Great Creator, no matter who or what they are. This is what is important. Sometimes it takes a while, but what I would like you to remember, my dear friend, is that each and everyone is entitled to the Love of those that they have known. So, I can truthfully say to you, my dear friend, that whoever this being is—and you must not use them in the past tense, they are *still with you*; they will have been loved and guided from the minute they passed to Spirit. So, I say to you: if you are involved in any way with those who become a little *fanatical* about their *religions*, just to gently remind them that we *all came from the same place and we will all return to the same place.* "

Salumet 2015/11/23

Physical pain in paradise?

Les: In the next world, is it possible for the

inhabitants to suffer?

You mean physically? *(Yes)* Of course not,
physically—they do not possess a *physical* body.
They can damage themselves, yes, but it is not a
physical damage, it is a *spiritual-emotional*
damage that they can create for themselves.

Les: I see. So, they wouldn't break a limb or
anything?

No, that is not possible. In their *minds* they can,
but of course, if they don't have a physical body,
they cannot have a physical brain, but the damage
can be there mentally, emotionally, and that is why
you do the 'rescues'. You are dealing with
emotionally damaged Spirit beings.

How about Insects and animals?

Les: I've heard that insects and butterflies are larger
and much more beautiful than in this world and
become very friendly if you wish them to be?

It would depend. Yes, all things are, shall we say,
'larger than life', as you would know it. But when
you are speaking of insect life—butterflies, bees,
flies, whatever you wish to speak of—unless they
have the contact here in a physical form, then what
would happen is they return to a group soul. There
are a few, and this I know, this is what you are
speaking of—those would appear to be much
larger, much brighter, than you would find here on
your Earth, but the majority return to the group
soul.

In the same way, we are asked about pets, the
animals, the dogs, the horses, the cats—the same

245

applies.

<u>Les:</u> So, they would not have Souls as we would imagine?

They do, if they have been in touch with humankind—if they have found the expression of Love. That is what *singularises* them.

<u>Les:</u> So, if a former owner wishes to have his or her pet returned to them, then that can be?

If the pet has gone before, then it will be waiting for that owner—always remember it is the *Love* tie—that cannot be extinguished.

<u>Les:</u> So, they are in *'suspense'*, until the one who loves them calls?

Not necessarily so. They will have the freedom of the fields. They will have the Love of other people, if that is what they so wish, but yes, they will be there—they will wait for that Love tie, when the time is right. Yes, let me say this to you: When you leave your physical beings, *all*, all *THOUGHTS become reality.* You can have whatever you want to. If you wish to see a field of horses, a field of sheep, whatever—the thought will make that materialise for you. So again, we come back to the *POWER of your THOUGHTS*

Salumet 1994/08/08

246

Next, *(2012/11/12)* Sister Wendy from a Silent Order, *(when on Earth)* shares her afterlife experience:

Yes—I really don't feel that you can appreciate such beauty. If you take something beautiful here, then you really have to triple it I would say—it's *BEAUTIFUL!*

Paul: And we understand there's a wider range of *colours* than the range normally seen here?

Yes, you will see hues of colour not known here on this Earth. Yes, I can confirm that for you—even the water is full of sound and colour.

Rod: Does it rain for the flowers and plants?

There is no need! But sometimes we have people who have looked after plants on this planet, and *think* that they need to be *watered*—so of course, whatever they desire, that is their reality. But they soon realise there is no need.

Paul: And when you meet people, everything is *revealed*—they cannot hide who they are?

There is nothing that is not known—you cannot be *false* in any way.

Paul: That's so nice, because *'down here'* so many people—like politicians talk about one thing, whilst thinking and intending different...

Yes, many of your people are like 'Janus'. *[The Roman god facing both ways at once!]*

Paul: Ah yes—it's such a *two-faced* world, I think. It must be so nice, when you meet someone and see exactly what they're about!

Yes of course. Remember, you will only be drawn to those you are compared to—the same kind of people—you will not be so different. It is nice to see that openness, that honesty and Love.

George: I was interested in what you said about the *sound* in water. (Yes) I once had a wonderful *'raised awareness'* experience in a *Mayan temple* (Yes) and somewhere within it there was a *water-drip.* I put my ear to the wall and the *water-drip* seemed to have many, many *musical notes!*

Yes, it was singing to you! Yes, it was singing to you and that experience is something that is common-place in Spirit. Yes, people stand under beautiful waterfalls for healing, because of their colours and their sounds.

Sara: And do the flowers sing as well?

Yes, everything *SINGS!* I think perhaps a better word would be *resonance*—but it is like the flowers are singing.

Sara: Every colour has a sound resonance?

Yes it does, in the same way as your names do here, have a resonance to you.

(We chatted about the effect of music on plants, explaining how they can show more growth when melodious music is played.)

All plants would respond in some way, but perhaps not in the way that you would expect.

Paul: Like us!

Yes, listening to a piece of music, you may all have differing opinions.

Paul: Everything is one and the same really, whether it is a *plant*, *human* or an *animal*—everyone wants *music that is beautiful.*

Yes, even people who say they do not like music—they still respond to it—it is wonderful to see the response.

Paul: Salumet mentioned how music can be a very effective way to help *depressed people*, to get them *'out'* of themselves.

I see, yes—music can carry you to another place, in the same way that the silence did for me. That is what I got from going into the silence. *(Referring to her silent Order of Nuns, during her Earth life.)*

George: So, do you enjoy having conversations with people now?

Well, I think I have proved that this evening! I don't think I have stopped talking! That's quite unusual. *(Chuckles)*

George: In Spirit also, do you enjoy conversations with others in Spirit?

Well, shall I tell you something? I often meet with those Sisters with whom I shared the convent—and just for, shall I say 'devilment's sake,' we talk!

George: You are making up for the silence!

We are making up for the silence! Although we were all of us extremely happy, but we meet sometimes just to talk.

(Rod asked if she had seen the film 'The Sound of Music'. No, but she would now be looking into that!)

Rod: You can just switch it on, can you?

Of course! I can do whatever I want to. I may even collect some of the Sisters and watch it together! *(Sara then referred to a concert and coincidently, she was thinking of singing a song from the movie.)* Lovely! Everyone should sing!

Rod asked about her present work—she teaches children—the teaching is not stressful/problematical like on earth. It brings her great joy and there's much singing! Rod asked if they learn complex subjects, like algebra and trigonometry?

They learn the kinds of things they would have done here, but they also learn spiritual things, hand-in-hand—it goes together.

<u>Paul:</u> *Mm,* the way it *should be!*

Yes, but the children have a very *special Light* and they *enjoy* learning! I think that is not always the case on Earth. *(Agreed)* But the Spirit children just can't wait to learn. And I have to tell you that I have been blessed both in the life that I had as a *Sister* and in the life that I lead now!

The next guest was arranged by Salumet: Catherine the Great—1762-1796, shares her reflections:

Your silence and expectation is commendable. I am so pleased to be here with you. I have to admit that all at this particular moment in time does seem confusing. But hopefully it should clear and I will be able to give you the information that I intended to

give. I was not prepared for this confusion of
thought, on entering this life.

Les: I understand that it is very confusing at first,
when one returns to the *physical*—it does *clear*, as the
voice continues to be used.

Yes, I am happy with the instrument, *(Eileen)* but it
is like swimming through a sea of fog, at this
moment. But I will try to recall, if you will bear with
me.

Les: Is there anything we can concentrate on, to assist
you?

I ask only for your Love please.

Les: We can certainly give you that.

It is strange to be touching such rough material.

Les: Yes, I suppose it must be rough to you now.

Yes, it is not unpleasant, but strange. I was not
prepared for it, so please bear with me and we will
begin our conversations shortly. I am also trying to
adjust the voice, because I know it is not how I
would wish it to be.

Les: No, it is quite clear...

If you are happy with it, then we could continue.
(Agreed) Then do you know why I have been sent to
you?

Les: No, Salumet said that we would have somebody
coming, who we would find to be very interesting...

I am deeply touched that those words should have
been used about me. But of course, the reason
behind my returning is the teaching that you have
received—that I am in fact a 'cut off,' of the

personality, of the whole, which is returning in different time and different body. It is not that we wish to impress, but that we wish to give details. We do not need to give you evidence, of life after your so-called 'death'. That is not why we return, because you have gone further than that. So, the reason behind this return visit, is to show you that the personality can cut itself off from the whole, and make a return.

I will try to bring forward some facts, as you may bring to memory and help you to recognise who I am.

Les: Good. You probably are aware that we do record everything?

I am not familiar with your recording machines, but I have been told of this. Let me say to you all, it is good to be amongst an audience once again. This happened many times, in the lifetime, which I have come to speak to you about. It was quite normal for me and I accepted it too easily, as being the norm. So once again to be amongst a group of people, does indeed seem strange, because of course, as I have gone on in this side of life, I know how unnecessary this was. But of course, it was my life's plan, at that particular time and I do accept it now. Firstly, I would like to give you my name, although I do realise that you probably will not recognise it. I was known as *Sophia Auguste Friederike.*

Les: Really—thank you, I *DO* recognise it.

You do? But of course, to others throughout the world, I would have been better known as *Catherine.* But I have to say here and now, I always objected to changing my name. And always I was known as Sophia, when I came to this side of life. I rather resented the intrusion on my birth name, but being a young woman, I had no say in these matters of state.

Les: Unfortunately in your time, that was so, wasn't it?

Indeed it was, and of course I was a young snip-of-a-girl, and did not dare to speak out.

Les: No, I imagine you do very differently now, where you are now?

This is what I come to tell you. All of your life's troubles do not mean so much when you come to the larger side of life. Everything comes into perspective—you see your life's plan, you see the pitfalls and you see the good points of it all, and of course you learn from your many lives. You understand this of course. *(Agreed)* I have been instructed that you have been told much. So, an evening of this kind, I believe, is light-hearted for you?

Les: I find it very interesting nevertheless, particularly when somebody such as yourself comes to speak to us.

I had much to regret when I left this life, or at least the life I am speaking of, because in your yearly terms, many years have gone by. But I speak only of this time, in order that you can make recognition, for yourselves and to understand that time is of the least importance, when it comes to the continuity of your lives.

Les: Yes, this we are beginning to understand. Incidentally, your voice is now very much clearer. It is clearing. We were hoping that the control would have been greater this time, but we must always work with what we have. It is strange how these things become misty. You would assume that all would be natural in memory, but it is not so. I am recalling just a few times of this lifetime, which I can tell you about. They obviously made a great impact in my life when I lived here. So, may I tell you a little?

Les: Please do! You undoubtedly are aware of the intense silence—everybody's anxious to hear you. My childhood was mainly uneventful. I believe I was a loved child, but my mother had great promises made for me. Her ideal was to see me married well. So, this is how my name came to be changed, much to my annoyance at the time. The decision in my life, was made firstly in 1744—this is the time we go back to, because this is my first strong memory. When I was taken from my homeland, small duchy from Germany, influenced I might say, by Frederic, who was a strong powerful man at the time—I was transported by my mother to Russia. I have to tell you, I was terrified at the prospect. I was a petite young woman, aged only 15

of her years. Can you imagine what it must have felt like, to be transported from one's homeland and bosom of your family, to be confronted by a woman so strong, so powerful, that not one word was uttered in her presence?

Les: That was Irena?

The empress. I have to tell you, she was not unkind to me, but she did not show affection either. To one so young, it was indeed disturbing, and distressing.

Les: I can imagine. Why did they take you there?

Because I was to become betrothed to the empress's nephew.

Les: I see, thank you. It must have been a ghastly experience for you.

I was instructed in Russian language, which I have to say at that time distressed me. I was instructed in the orthodox religion; I was instructed in the court ways—in so many things in such a short space of time. Also, my name was changed to Catherine and I was betrothed to Peter. He was a thin gangly pock-marked young boy, only one year older than I, but I would happily have joined him with love, if only he could have shown me some affection, but that was never to be. The memory now distresses me, when I think back to the love I left behind, within my own family background.

Les: Were you never able to visit your family?

My mother stayed with me and frequently wrote back to my father all progress made, but I was so unhappy. But I could never show it, because of course I was constantly told how great an honour was being bestowed upon me, that one day I would become a great lady. I never wanted that, but fate and circumstances were due to bring me just that. I am speaking to you now, about the human element of this woman; I am speaking to you about the feelings within her heart that were never spoken aloud at the time, because she was a woman so young in age, she was *TERRIFIED* to say one word out of place. (Yes) The next memory that comes to me, is of the marriage ceremony. I was taken to the empress's home, where she took charge to dress me, to bejewel me, to instruct me. And so both Peter and I were transported to the great cathedral, to the 'Virgin of Kassam.' I remember thinking how appropriate that name was and how terrified I was to become the wife of this 17-year-old boy.

Les: We can quite understand it must have been a terrible experience.

The cathedral was beautiful, and will always be imprinted on my memory. It took several hours, of course I don't know how much you know of the Russian courts in those days, but such a wedding, was indeed spectacular. We returned to banquet and feast. Can you imagine *so* much food, but the worst part for me, was the obligation to dance with so many old noble-men—I was *horrified.* Even now I can *feel* myself quake from this old memory.

Les: Are you not able to clear these old memories and give yourself peace of mind?

Of course, they have been gone through, it is only the return to this physical world, which brings with it, not only the memories, but the pain of them. Of course, they have gone, when I leave here, they will be gone forever. (Good.) I only bring them to you, to bring some authenticity to my memory. I am not in pain now, you understand? *(Agreed)* But the memory is so strong.

Les: I asked the question, because we did have someone from an earlier age than yours even, who told us that her visit enabled her to clear her mind completely of traumas...

No, I have none of those problems, I fully accepted when I came to this side of life, I knew what I had done, what I had done wrong and I knew what had to be done. There are many memories within a lifetime, which have to be faced up to. And I will tell you now, because it took me many, many of your years' time, to fully accept what I had done. Although I did not actually raise my own hand, I was responsible for Peter's death.

Les: Were you?

Of course, those in court circles saw me distressed when the news came, but I knew in my heart that is what his fate would be. You see by then I had become a worshipped lady throughout the lands. The people wanted me to rule, because Peter was a weak and infantile man and I have to say his mind was not fully there. He was subject to many stormy outbursts and he did not please the people, because he was in favour of Frederick, who was a powerful—in Peter's mind, 'ally.' And all the Russian people, they could see that he could not be a good and strong ruler. Do you see, the power came to me, without even my soul wishing or desiring it to begin with? (Yes) But once, ONCE you have the adrenaline flowing through your veins, once you have the feel of the POWER and the adoration of your peoples, then your life can take a turn for the worse. This I had to face up to. I had MUCH to face up to. *(Agreed)* But he was an unfeeling and unloving young man, but I was a warm-hearted, pretty young woman, who desired the love of a man. I do not deny this, neither do I feel grief about it, because circumstance you see, dictated always that I find love. I have to say and I must say to you, that it is not well known or understood, that Peter fully accepted our child as his own. In fact, my three children belonged to different men, this I am not sorry for, because I loved each and every one of them. But I have to say, if life could have been different, I would have chosen another pathway.

Les: Yes—you didn't wish for the power ....

I did not and when I looked back over that lifetime, I could see I had done much good. For the people close by, I had fond memories and not least my own son. And that was my parting memory and one which caused me continuous grief for a long time, because although my peoples called me, 'Catherine

258

the Great,' to my own son I was neither a good mother, nor heroine. He despised me, because you see, he always believed Peter to be his true father. So, on my death, he instructed that Peter's remains be dug up and that both of us would go together. And he instructed *(Spoken with tears/unclear/faint on audio)* Alex's father to carry both of us also—if only he had known that Alexis was the father *(of my loved one?)* he would indeed have been shocked. You cannot imagine what it was like to watch this from this side of life and to be unable to comfort him?

<u>Les:</u> It must have been a terrible time for you.

It was, but it opened my eyes to what I had to accept.

<u>Les:</u> But I believe I'm right that though you didn't wish for the power, mainly you used it for the benefit of your people?

My peoples were so glad, because as I have said, Peter would have sided with Frederick of Prussia and he *(Frederick)* would have eventually turned against us, but he could not see this. He was a simple man, with little strength, little true knowledge, and so I had to take control, not only for the peoples, but for the future of Russia. I have since spoken with Peter, who has told me he also was afraid and we were both so young. He also was like a little boy. All he wanted to do was to play with his soldiers, in his gardens, with his toys. He was not ready for manhood, to rule a great country,

or to take a wife. These things also came to him—
you have to understand that in those times, you
had no say in what your fate was to be.

Les: No, but it would seem it was necessary to take
the part you did in that life, because of Peter's short-
comings.

I understand that now, it is the one thing I have
accepted. I reigned for 34 years, of your time and I
do say to you, most of them were good. I
developed from a petite soft young woman, into a
woman of strength, of knowledge, capable of great
love. And to say I truly loved the first man I had my
first child with—there was no-one to match him,
but he was sent away, for diplomatic purposes,
because of the rumours it caused.

Les: I see, so that happiness was taken from you
also?

I know now, it was this that made me strong. I then
looked to guiding my son and to trying to influence
Peter, who ignored me and had no love for me at
all. And he also could see that he too was at fault,
but he was simple in his mind and at times very
destructive with his words, though all was forgiven
at the time. And I have to say that since that
lifetime, my heart has been heavy, not only for
what has happened in Russia, but in my homeland
of Germany. But I think I would be right in telling
you that the nations of your world, are becoming
much more sensible, that they are beginning to
recognise that love for all mankind. *(Agreed)* I do

believe I must depart now. I thank you for allowing this time, I thank you for the opportunity of memory, I thank you and I say to you all:

Love one another as you would those closest to you. Know that all in your lives can be good, if you so desire.

<u>Les:</u> We hope you can be happy now—isn't that possible for you?

I am happy, I am happy. I do this only because it is instructive for you. All my memories have disappeared in the life that I now lead. I am only a small fragment of that life which exists now.

<u>Les:</u> Well, we do thank you for having come here tonight and for what you've told us. We can only say that our *full Love* goes with you.

(Very faint—she seems to refer again to her first-love.)

I did love Sergey, I did. I loved him from the very first part of my being—he was a truly great man and he deserved the title 'great,' **not** Peter, not Peter, not Peter ...

Thank you *Sophia* foer sharing memories of what was a difficult life, in spite of wealth and '*high status*'. Who would want to sit on a *golden throne*, in a *ceremonial life*, unable to run free and be with *true Love?*

What do you suppose would be your Heaven upon Earth within your present time?

George: Heaven is to do with our stronger Soul-connection—the stronger that connection, the more *'heaven-aware'* we are. It is such a wonderful Earth and one can look to the wonderful aspects of it and *see* it as Heaven, or *heavenly.*

Yes—Heaven comes from *within*—this you know. To those of you with some degree of spiritual knowledge, it is easy for you to see around you many aspects of this Earth, which is endowed with *Heavenly Creation*, but to the majority of Earth-kind, they are still focussed in this time of your evolution, upon the disputes of mankind, the greed within your world, the many *'disasters'* as you call them—and in doing so, they overlook how much mankind has grown, they overlook the beauty and the joy of existence. The beauty and the joy of existence belongs to each individual, it is an individual attribute, which each one of you carries within. Each one of you my dear friends, I have told you before, is like a *beacon of Light*—so, each individual one is a little part of Heaven upon this Earth.

If each individual light was to join together to make *ONE*, then indeed that vision of Heaven upon this Earth would indeed be much brighter than at any time of earthly existence. Many would dispute these words, many would say, *'but there is*

so much hatred, so much greed, so much violence'. But as you do, my dear friends, they will reach a point when all of those things become insignificant. What is important is that the light shines from within, in order that that *Sea of Light* can flow further and further upon your Earth.

Salumet 2003/10/13

We are *Beings of Love* and *t*here are *infinite supplies*—the more *we GIVE*, the more *flows* back to *YOU*, on this *'Sea of Light' voyage that Salumet describes*—our *spiritual avatars* are awakening—it's on the *horizon of our THOUGHTS,*

"In helping just *one* person, *one person,* with *Love* in your hearts, with unselfishness and no thought for self, then you are beginning to achieve *true spiritual worth.*"

Salumet 1998/08/03

And on that note, it's time to say farewell along this supercali-spiritualistic journey, bubbling with Love and Light and happy in the knowledge that one day we WILL all return HOME and LIVE outrageously blissfully ever after!

Appendix 1:

The Light Escort and the Tunnel of Light

This guest was arranged by *Salumet* and channelled by *Eileen*. A *'Tunnel-of-Light'* worker, known as **'The Light Escort'**, provides knowledge about the transition from *Earth to Spirit*:

Firstly, I am **glad to join you all. I have been aware of this moment for some time, for which much preparation has taken place. Salumet thought you would be interested in hearing what I do within our world. In fact I do more than one job, I think you would say. But mainly, I am an 'Escort of Light.' Do you understand what that is?**

<u>Les:</u> Not completely.

I'm being told, no they do not, that is why you were sent. (*Laughter*) **Right—I'm finding myself now. Yes, what I do and what I mean by an escort of light, perhaps you will recognise if when I say I am the unseen beam of light, when people travel the tunnel of light. I am the vision of light that awaits the passing.**

<u>Les:</u> Oh, that's lovely and we do thank you for the effort you put into this. We've heard about it so many times.

I think we are the unknown entities of the Spirit world. So many times, when these things are recalled, we are referred to as, 'I think I felt and could feel someone there, but we were not sure.' Yes, and people feel and think they see something, but are never sure. Well, I have to tell you I am not unknown, I am real.

Les: Yes, we quite believe that. And so that is your main task, is it?

That is my main mission, yes.

Les: Yes, mission is a better word. You don't consider it a task?

It is no task, it is work, it is growth, it is unending *Love.*

Les: Why is it necessary to have a tunnel? Is that to direct and conduct energies in the two planes of life?

Yes, it is to buffet the Soul. It would be too much of a shock, too much of an energy shock for the Spirit. It needs to be buffeted and that is the reason why most, I would not say all, but most people feel that Love energy surround them.

You see, within this so-called tunnel, it is energy of Love, I prefer to call it. It is seen as a tunnel, because of the state of the Soul, at a particular transition stage. That is all—we remain mainly unseen, because the Soul at that time, needs to be protected.

To those of a little more awareness, I sometimes appear as a very, very dull image, of what they assume is a person, but they are never sure. It very much depends on the awareness of the passing Spirit.

Les: So, you can appear in a varying degree of light or dimness, according to the ability of the Soul to accept what it is experiencing at that time?

Yes, as you know while in your physical being that all of you vary in your degrees of awareness. Then that is how you perceive the tunnel of light and us—escort beings of Love. It is all to do with spiritual awareness.

Les: I see. I think I would be right in saying that it is not necessary for every Soul to pass through that tunnel?

Of course not, some find themselves immediately in our side of life. It is not something that is experienced by all, by any means. But of course, we know of those who will experience this and thereby our task becomes imminent, you see?

Les: Yes, you adjust accordingly, to the one who is about to enter.

You see in the in-between state, of what you term, 'life' and 'death,' sometimes it is necessary for us to show ourselves as a bright light.

Les: Yes—that would overcome I imagine, any attempt there is, not to leave this plane. The fact that there is a bright light would attract a reluctant Soul?

Yes, of course. That is one of the objects of it, that there are those within their bodies, who will fight to the very last, to remain within their physical overcoats, you see?

Les: I see, thank you. And going back to the fact that some do not need to pass through the tunnel, I refer to my own wife's comment, when she came over, that there was what she described as a puff of wind and then she found herself in your plane of life.

Yes—let me say, what or who do you suppose is the puff of wind? I have many guises. You see whichever way, whatever happens in the transition stage, we are always there, whether we are known of, seen or unseen.

Les: Yes, I would imagine she was feeling an enfoldment of Love, to welcome her.

Yes, and you say those words beautifully. We are an *'enfoldment of Love'*—that is what I am. I feel so emotional, when I say those words, whilst using a physical voice. It is something of beauty. I have experienced much—much joy, much sadness from those on your side of life. But mainly the joy it brings to those who work together, really is something to behold.

Les: Yes. I think we are quite unable to imagine the extent of joy that is possible in your world.

You cannot. One day perhaps you will, but we speak of such a long time of development, before you could achieve such bliss. *(Agreed)*

I am being told to say to you a little of how those of us are chosen, to do this work.

Les: That would be most interesting for us to know.

Forgive me if I don't seem forthcoming, but it is strange for me to sit within a physical body, trying

268

to express what is—I don't know—seems so beyond your understanding.

<u>Les:</u> It must be difficult for you.

So, I am being prompted to tell you a little more. We come from a state of what I can only term, '*Supreme Love*'. I believe you term it this—that is the closest word.

<u>Les:</u> Yes, I think that is the closest we can get to it. Once that stage is reached then there are many options open to us. I will speak a little of what I felt, at the time of deciding of how I wanted to continue with my growth. I was listening to a gathering of many, when one speaker stepped forward, who would give to me inspiration for what I had to do. I had a choice. I could continue as I was—I could teach others, many who would come and gather around me, to teach. By this I was most humbled; but henceforth came this speaker of light, and approach me he did. And without going into too much detail, he showed me that the way to go was to come back, not as someone visible and known, who would be grateful for such things, but to return through many spheres, to help those who are lost, who are lonely and who need help. Can you understand how shattering this realisation was to me?

<u>Les:</u> Yes, I think I can.

Because you see, I suppose even in the state of bliss, there existed an element of vanity.

<u>Les:</u> That must have been shattering.

269

Not vanity as you would imagine the word to mean. But you see, to have people come to you, for you to teach, is a very great privilege. And—I don't know the word to express to you—I, in my ignorance, I suppose, thought that this was my Soul's way of growth. So, I was left for a time, to reconsider, because I have said to you it was my choice. I had the choice and I realised that this was the way I must go. So, you see, to become an Escort of Light, not to be seen, not to be recognised, but to have someone know that you are something, was indeed a very big experience for me.

Les: Yes, I'm sure it must have been. And you mentioned coming back through the spheres—about coming back to lower spheres, if I can use that expression, does not have to be a permanent condition for you, does it?

Not at all, not at all.

Les: No, you go back to your own sphere, which you have earned.

I return often, to replete to replenish, to be amongst those I should be with. I need to do this— we all need to do it. I think you would term it, *'to recharge your battery'*, yes? *(Gentle laughter)* Someone just told me, *'Say that and you'll be fine.'*

Les: That's right, we perfectly understand that expression.

Yes, it's quite a comparison, don't you think? I am telling you, I'm a *being of light* and I need to *charge my battery!* *(More laughter)* Yes, I'd rather forgotten

270

how amusing you beings could be—I have long forgotten. That is not to say we do not have our fun—of course we do.

Les: No, of course not, I'm glad you do. So, you periodically go back and then come down through the spheres again, to become an *Escort of Light*, for a given period, (Yes) until you feel the need to return to the place, which you have earned so far.

Yes. There is no set time. The need is known—the need to return is known.

Les: It would be known and you would be taken back.

This I believe, is something you don't know much about, that all needs, all time is known. We do not set clocks, we do not use calendars, but all is known.

Les: Yes, all is known. We cannot understand it, but we quite accept it.

Let me speak a little more. I hope I am not taking too much of your time?

Les: Good heavens no, you can go on as long as you wish.

You are most kind. (Pause) Ah yes, someone is saying, '*Do not procrastinate, go on speaking.*' (*Laughter*) Sorry if I am doing that, I don't mean to.

Les: No, we are really thrilled to have you speaking to us like this and I don't use that word lightly.

Thank you, I do feel your warmth. Let me speak a little, let me tell you what happens to those souls, who are buffeted by us. We escort them to the area, I think you would say—their 'destination'.

Les: Yes, the one they have fitted themselves for, in their physical life?

No, no, let me explain. Their destination, when they first arrive in our side of life. They are greeted mainly, by those who are known to them, for recognition purposes. If not, they are met by those who have helped to keep them safe, throughout their earthly life. But in any case, there is someone, who to the being just arrived, who is solid—rather than we who are unseen, they can see, they can feel, they can touch, if they so wish.

Les: They can identify more fully and more confidently with those people, I understand.

Yes, but this is not where they are destined to be, because before that happens, they have to have a re-run of their earthly lives. Much has been spoken on this. Once this happens, then we withdraw and they are left in the hands of those who are there to help them.

Les: And those people would be nearer to the physical plane, than you can be?

Yes. We help them, but we leave them, when they actually leave the earthly realm, you understand me?

(Yes) We then return to those who need us. Let me just say something, may I?

Les: Yes please.

So often, we hear those of you who say, 'I think I saw this, I think I saw that.' Most times they are not seeing anything spiritual, because when they do, there is no doubt, no doubt. So, can I say to you, I'm being hurried along, because I'm slowing down, I do believe, I'm not aware of it—am I slowing please?

Les: I wouldn't have thought so, no.

(Voice becomes fainter)

Thank you. When you see a spiritual light—those of us who work in that way, you will not doubt it—you will know it is the truth. If you have doubts, then by all accounts, it is not from Spirit. You understand me?

Les: I see, so the vision would make such an impact, that we would have no doubt about it being spiritual.

Yes, and that is why, when you have people who are close, who are ill, who see these spiritual lights, which no one else can, that is why they are so positive. That is why no one can persuade them otherwise. Do you see what I am telling you?

Les: Yes, so other visions which people have then, would be classified as clairvoyance would they, rather than spiritual visions?

Yes, yes, that's true, yes that is what I am trying to express to you. There would be no doubt, no doubt. Yes, it is not quite as easy as I'd presumed it would be, but nevertheless I hope I am giving you information not known to you.

273

Les: You certainly are doing that and we are extremely grateful to you.

When the tunnel of light is seen, it almost radiates down to the forehead of the being who is seeing the tunnel, and they are drawn—you know the Spirit leaves that way—I'm being told you have the knowledge of that. It travels up the tunnel which, if you can visualise, the energies are much heavier at the bottom. As the being travels closer to us, then the energies become much, much lighter.

Les: That would account for the fact that we have been told from a number of rescues, that their journey through the tunnel, suddenly becomes faster and faster.

Yes, and their experience as they come closer to Spirit side of life, there is more they feel and think they see, because of course on the lighter energies, much more work can be done. The closer we go to the denser energies, the more difficult it is, to help that Spirit being.

Les: As you are experiencing by talking to us tonight.

Yes, that is why I found it so difficult, but I must say the longer I stay, the easier it becomes.

Les: Good, I'm pleased to hear that.

Yes, now would you like to ask me anything?

Les: Yes, there is one question I'd like to ask you. You have said that all is known in your world and this we can accept. In what way are you given the information that a soul is approaching the time to go through the tunnel, or to reach your plane?

274

How do we know—because we see their light. We do not see you as human beings clothed within these bodies, heavy, heavy, heavy. No, we are attracted by the light energy, which become depleted.

Les: I see, so you know then that the time has come for that soul to take its journey to you.

Let us say it is not an instantaneous thing. If the knowledge is known, there are many preparations made. But of course, there are occasions on your earthly plane, where life ends as you would say, sooner than it should. In those instances, we are instructed by those higher beings of light, who have much more knowledge than we do.

Les: I see. I ask the question, because last night, 24 hours ago, I was asked by a communicator from one of the spheres nearer Earth, that if I wished to see a gentleman friend of long standing, whom I knew would not recover his health, I was asked to go and see him as quickly as possible. It occurred to me when that statement was made, that you must have the knowledge that they would soon be passing.

Yes, of course we do. That knowledge exists beforehand, as I have said, preparations are made, because let me explain a little to you—I'm being told to explain this a little more. When you are on the Earth as you are, when you are in full health, your energies shine out to us like beacons, pure light energy, because you are Spirit you see, we see the spiritual aspects of you, not the human heavy dense matter, you follow? (Yes) As those energies deplete, as illness comes upon you, so your colours, your energy, your light changes—subtly, slowly, slowly. So there comes a certain stage within your living, when we are aware that the time is near for you to join us; your colours and your lights inform us. It's rather like a magnet that attracts many to it, can you understand?

Les: Yes, I understand what you say, thank you.

That is how we are aware and I believe if you ask Salumet, he will explain that there are many whose task it is to do this work.

Les: To advise you of the imminent passing of somebody from this Earth?

Yes, but of course remember too, that those loved ones on the lower levels, who are closer to those they have left behind, are in constant touch and they also know when their time is near.

Les: So, they will have the knowledge to interpret the fading of the energy?

They will be aware, that is how the preparations can take place.

Les: And that is how relatives who have passed on, are able to appear to the one who is due to pass?

Yes, because you see the very fact of the energy depleting, is enough to draw those loved ones to that soul.

Les: Thank you, that's very clear.

Have I helped you in understanding?

Les: I think undoubtedly you have.

Because after all, that is what we are trying to impart to you.

Les: Yes, you have given us wonderful information tonight. There is one final question, I feel the power is going. (Yes) In the case of a person suffering an unexpected accident, we've always assumed their time on Earth has been cut short, because of that accident, it may or may not be so, it's difficult to say, perhaps their time had come—but in the case of somebody's life being cut short prematurely, am I right in saying they are 'cocooned' in some way until their time arises?

Yes, I understand your question. Not always, not always, it would depend on the period of time that lapsed between the passing and the intended natural passing, you follow?

Les: Yes, it would depend upon the amount of time still left?

Yes, let me give you an example, yes, Salumet is telling me this subject has been discussed, but he's telling me continue—Let me say to you, if you have a child, who really was destined to live much longer, if the period of the earthly years was one of long duration, then of course the child would be cocooned until such time, because you see, we have said it is a shock, you understand? So, you must not try to visualise your earthly years, you should not try to imagine time as you know it, because that does not work for you. If for instance, someone's passing takes place, shall we say, just a few years of your earthly time, then there is no reason why they should not go forward. They will be instructed, told of why that passing was sooner than it should have been.

Les: I see. Thank you that does clarify some points that had been in my mind, since we did discuss it with Salumet. I apologise to him, for bringing it up again, it wasn't that he didn't explain it fully, I'm sure he did, but it was simply a question in my own mind, and probably in the minds of my colleagues.

He is saying, that is why he comes, he wants you all to fully understand.

Les: Yes, well now we do. I'm sure it must have occurred to some of my friends here too, the same questions.

There are many, many difficult things for you to understand we know, but we try to help you.

Les: You are certainly unravelling an awful lot for us.

Yes well, I hope it has been instructive and you can give forth the information given to you, for those who feel they have travelled the tunnel and returned, who say they felt sure there was someone there, but they could not see them—

(Chuckles) Perhaps you will remember me and say, well we know who it could have been.

Les: Yes, we shall certainly remember you and we all thank you, don't we? (Affirmed)

May the Love of the Creator be with you all and I know I won't be seeing you just yet!

(Chuckles)

Les: We shall think of you doing your job anyway.

Peace and Love be yours.

And finally, one called Ernest, shared his simple, yet deep and thoughtful pointers, about the *Journey—(1998/01/12)*

I think you all think you know what will happen when you die and I'm here to tell you that you probably don't! (General agreement + chuckles)

Les: Yes, we've all got different ideas, I'm sure.

Yeah, most people do, but it's usually different from what they expect, or WHO they expect. Cos you all know you're gonna be met by somebody, don't you? (Agreed) *But it's not always who you think.*

Les: No, it's not always relatives, because of the emotion.

Yes, not only the emotion—it's not always true what you feel when you're living here. You might think it is, but it's not always. So sometimes it might be a bit of a shock. Well don't worry cos there's people like me standing by to help, especially when we've made some physical contact, while you're still alive—but you know all that I'm being told, somebody's saying, don't keep going over old ground. (Laughter) *They'll get bored.*

Les: No, no we shan't. So, you might be there to meet one of us?

279

*Well not meet you, but I might be standing by.
That's my job you see, helping in the beginning.*

Les: So, what does happen when we come over to you then?

*Depends on what you expect, depends on your last
minutes, depends on what you believe and it
depends who wants to meet you— (Laughter)
whether they've got other things to be doing. I
don't mean that, I'm just being—*

Les: They couldn't have anything better to do than meet us…

*Well let me tell you that's not true—(Laughter) not
that I want to disappoint you or anything—*

Les: No, I'm sure they'd have better things to do…

*But if they love you, yes, they'll meet you when the
time's right.*

Les: So, somebody meets us and then what do they do with us?

*Depends on you, again it depends on you and the
conditions in which you come to us. If it's been a
long illness, then you'll probably awake in one of
our hospitals.*

Les: Yes, and they're very nice, I've been shown them.

*Have you? Well, you're honoured to have been
allowed that. But of course, if that happens, you'll
have many loved ones around you, helping to bring
you back to full strength and energy, because
that's the natural progress of somebody who loves
you. But you'll be well protected, if that's the case.
But the most traumatic moment, is the moment
when you see everything before you.*

280

Les: Yes, when we see our own lives…

Yes, that's the traumatic part of any passing. And that's why we have people such as myself, to stand by to offer help if we're needed—only if we're needed.

Les: And to help us overcome the shock of what we've done?

To help buffet you and surround you and help you over—probably the shock, because most people are shocked at what they haven't done.

Les: Quite, what they haven't done, more than what they have done!

Yes, it's not what they have done, it's what they HAVEN'T done and all their missed opportunities.

Les: Yes, that can be a shock.

It's a very big shock I tell you and of course it's very traumatic for many; there are many tears, cos we do have tears; it's not all happiness to begin with. But that soon dispels and you go on, to where you should belong.

Les: And my friends and I know, that we go to a place suitable, that we have earned.

Oh yes, yes you can only go to what you're entitled to yes, yes. And I have to tell you that there are places that you wouldn't want to know about, but I'm not coming here to frighten you, because none of you'll be going there, if I can help it.

Les: Good, that's comforting to know.

Yes, the lady Dawn doesn't sound too sure? (Laughter) *Don't you worry my dear, I'll take your arm, don't you worry.*

<u>Dawn:</u> Jolly good.

Yes, never mind—

<u>Les:</u> And then we go to whatever place has been prepared for us?

Not straight away, you could meet other people you've known first, before that takes place. There's no set pattern, that's something else I've come to tell you. There are too many stories about this, that and the other happening. Remember that you're all very individual people and as such, you're dealt with in that way. There are certain factors which must be dealt with of course, but it depends what your desire and expectation is. You understand me?

<u>Les:</u> Yes, we do understand Ernest thank you. Yes, it's interesting what you're telling us.

Yeah, you remember that before you pass in most cases, that people are waiting for you.

<u>Les:</u> That's the main thing, isn't it?

Yes, people are waiting there for you, so it's only right, if that is what you're entitled to, that your loved ones meet you at some stage.

<u>Les:</u> Yes, and then after that, it's just like going obviously into a new...phase of existence?

Probably one of your loved ones will introduce you to your new place of abode.

<u>Les:</u> Which they no doubt will have got ready for us, *(Yes)* according to the materials we have sent them.

It all depends on how you've lived your lives.

<u>Les:</u> That's it. *(Yes)* That's what I mean, if we don't send them the spiritual material, they can't prepare a place for us.

Of course not; I wish more people could understand that, yes.

Les: Only a few evenings ago here, I had somebody investigating our work and he was surprised when I told him it wasn't all roses, milk and honey there.

If you think that, then I'm afraid you're in for a BIG shock, big shock, big shock.

Les: They are I know; that's why I tell them.

Yes, people expect everything to change, when in fact very little changes to begin with. You'll still be YOU, just without your old body.

Les: That's it, our personality continues, just as it is here.

Yes, yes, same as I've still got mine, you see? Yes, I still use my old name when I come back, don't I?

Les: Yes, you don't need to use that where you are though.

No, but you don't forget it, do you?

Les: No, you don't.

Anyway, that's what I came to tell you. Don't have any set ideas and you'll accept those conditions much more readily.

Les: I am right though I think, in saying that the soul can reproduce the physical body without any complaints, illnesses or diseases, that sort of thing, but a spiritual replica of the physical body, for recognition?

Yes of course, yes, that's the power of the thought—that is SPIRIT, it's THOUGHT—a land of thought—that's what it is. Not everyone can manage to capture that to begin with. It takes time sometimes, to discard that old body; to realise that you don't need a voice and you don't need physical things.

Les: No, we do a lot of *rescue work* here, for people who are in that sort of condition.

Oh, I see, that's very good work, that's very good work.

Les: We do a great deal of it here; we're pleased to be able to.

Yes, there's lots of it needed I'm told, yes.

Les: There certainly are some poor souls over there, in need of help.

Yes, we have those who help those in need on my side of life, of course there is, there's got to be, otherwise we'd be in a poor way, wouldn't we?

Les: We certainly would. We've all got to help each other, in whatever way we can.

Yes, of course you must. That's what it's all about.

Les: How do you spend your time mainly Ernest? What do you do?

I've just said, I'm there to help those newcomers. Somebody's telling me you've been told before, about going through the tunnel, that there are recognisable shadows. Sometimes that's part of my duty as well, but mainly I'm at the other end of the tunnel, when you've arrived and the confusion and the traumatic experiences. I'm there to help and guide and protect.

Les: Yes, somebody told us that they show themselves as lights in the tunnel.

Yes, but sometimes souls recognise them as outlines of people. It depends on their own spiritual knowledge of course. But yes, it's visible

within that tunnel of light, yes, yes. So that's
mainly my tasks.

<u>Les:</u> So, everybody has to go through that tunnel,
irrespective of the way in which they pass?

Not always—that's the main function of passing.
It depends if it's traumatic, sudden passing, then it
could be that they just find themselves on the other
side.

<u>Les:</u> I'd wondered about that.

Yes, it's not—it depends if it's a sudden death or
an expected death for that person, then it may just
be that they're confronted by someone, who's
waiting for them.

<u>Les:</u> Then comes the difficulty of persuading them.

Yes, at least if you're travelling through the tunnel
of Love, then you're being prepared for that
transition. But no, that's what I say, you shouldn't
expect just one happening, because there's many
ways of passing.

<u>Les:</u> Of course, we don't know in what way we are
going, when the time comes.

No, so don't be surprised and don't have fixed
ideas about what should happen.

<u>Les:</u> Well, that gives us a lot to think about and adds
to our knowledge considerably Ernest. *(Good.)* So, if
you hear us shouting for you, you'll know who it is.

Well don't all be shouting at once, will you?

<u>Les:</u> Oh, I don't suppose we'll all go at once.

I hope not—I don't mind keeping busy, but that's
ridiculous. (Laughter)

Anyway, I'll wish you all good luck in your lives
and I hope that you all carry on to the very best of

285

your abilities, because that's all you can do. You can't do more; just try your very best.

Les: That's all, just as you did tonight in coming through.

Yes, with a lot of difficulty.

Les: But you surmounted them and you're glad you did, I hope.

I'm pleased to have spoken to you all, yes, yes.

Les: It's been very nice to have you Ernest and we do thank you a lot.

Just take care of YOU, and THANK YOU, for allowing me here.

Appendix 2:

Meditation

"What is meditation? It is prayer, but it is prayer which is seeking that *within.* It is not external it is a prayer of trying to know yourself. Therefore, in meditation you are allowing the human aspect of you as you know yourself now, to be forgotten and the Soul to come forward. You go deep within that spiritual light, that spiritual knowledge which has the answer to all questions. Therefore, I say to you, to meditate is the answer to all things, all things spiritual."

Salumet 1999/11/08

Salumet's advice/guidance on meditation link:

**www.salumetandfriends.org/app/download/50308
89/SALUMET%2BMEDITATION%2BGUIDE.pdf**

Preparing for Meditation:

Meditation needs a **safe space** in which to *open to Spirit,* where you can completely *'unplug'* from the physical world and *'plug'* into *Source.* So, it needs to be done at an appropriate time, when there will be *no interruptions.* It's best to make it a **regular daily practise,** ideally, somewhere reserved for meditation/healing/energy work—In time, *sacred spaces* with purer energy are created.

On the Earth, the sun only shines during the day and sometimes there are clouds, but in meditation, the *Spiritual Sun* is shining bright *24/7* and is available whenever we wish!

All the meditation links below can be freely downloaded from the website and saved onto your device, so that you don't need to be *online* when *listening*. When opening up in meditation and spiritual work in general, it's always important to **ask for protection**: There are *dark entities* who are *not 'evil'* but more like *'wayward beings'* who choose to stay within dense, negative energy until the awareness is there to change. They can be attracted by our lights when opening ourselves. They can be repelled by sending Love and Light, but it's best to get into a routine of asking for protection before beginning:

<u>Protecting yourself:</u>

You can imagine being safely wrapped in a **Cloak of Light** or **Bubble of Love**. *We* always say something like: '**I open myself *only* to the LOVE AND TRUTH of Great Spirit/God, and ask for *protection* from *my guides and Great Spirit/God*'**—this works like a *spiritual 'firewall'*, such that only *Love and Truth* can get through. We really do have many watching over us, standing guard, but we shouldn't take their help for granted and it's always good to *ASK* and give *THANKS* for all their protection and guidance.

At the end of meditation or spiritual work in general, it's important to close down, much like when we awaken from a deep sleep, say *THANK YOU* to Spirit—maybe gently stretch and give yourself a little rub, drink some water and feel refreshed and fully awake.

All of these meditations and more can be found on the website:

http://www.SalumetandFriends.org/book-meditations/

Salumet guides a meditation of healing. (2016/08/01—5 minutes) –

One through Eileen takes us on a Meditative journey into healing waters to erase worries: (2022/01/10—9 minutes)

Another through Eileen takes us on a meditative journey to meet someone. (2022/09/12—13 minutes)

One through Eileen takes us on a meditative journey up golden steps. (2019/12/02—10 minutes)

Salumet takes us on a guided meditation: Opening to the White Light—connecting to Spirit. (6 minutes—2007/09/24)

Graham takes us on a meditative journey to the diamond tree of healing. (2023/11/13—7 minutes)

Sara takes us on a 'Joie de vivre' journey opening the Heart. (2023/07/22—4 minutes)

Leslie Bone takes us on a longer meditative walk through a Spirit Garden. *(1995/05/10—30 minutes)*

Spirit Garden meditative walk also available in *French*—read/translated by Sabine *(30 minutes)*

I invite you all if you wish, to join me now for a walk through one of our gardens. Would you care to follow me? Please be aware that you are barefooted—for this walk, you will not need shoes, or other coverings for your feet—that would destroy in part, your enjoyment of the walk. Please take off all footwear and leave at the gate.

Are you ready now?

Now you see a pair of gates, which are apparently golden, but are so-coloured only because this would be expected in conformity with the beauty, which they separate from the normal vista outside.

Now we go through the open gates, then you will see that the path upon which we now walk, is what you would call grass, but is no way similar to the grass of which you are aware upon your Earth.

Feel the grass with your feet—this is the reason for discarding your footwear. You should feel the energy coming through the Earth and the grass as you walk and you should also become aware that as you walk, your bodies are becoming lighter and lighter and that it requires no effort from your muscles to transport yourself along this path.

Are you beginning to feel that?

Do not worry if you cannot feel it exactly as I have described. It may be more apparent to you as we progress. We have only just started this walk. Now we come to an archway in the hedge, and the hedge as you would see, is not green as upon your Earth, but is multi-coloured, in all shades that you can imagine, and those colours change as you approach. The hedge is a living thing and the doorway is reacting to your own auras as you approach.

As you enter through the archway into the garden of roses, you will feel a warmth descending on you, which disappears again, as you go through the archway.

Are you able to feel that warmth?

Do not be concerned if you do not. Remember you are taking a physical body through a spiritual garden, therefore you may not feel all that we would wish you to feel; but it should be registered in your mind, so that later you can retrace your steps, if you wish. Now let us go through the garden of roses. Imagine every rose, which you have seen in the course of your lifetime all spread before you in a sea of colour, blossoming as you have never seen flowers blossom here. And the perfume, which arises from them all, is individual to each bush, but is an amalgam such as you have never experienced here. Try to inhale that marvellous mixture of perfume, it will cleanse your lungs, it will cleanse your Spirit, and give you energy for the continuation of the walk.

Look around you at the roses, enjoy the scent they give you.

Then I will take you through the aisle, which you would call a passage. Look down at the path beneath your feet now. What do you see? Golden sand of a texture so fine that you could not imagine it. And yet it does not swirl up in dust clouds as such a texture would upon the Earth. That path is energy, energy, energy, which can be transformed, transposed through your feet, into your very being. That is why it is so fine, so that it can be taken into your very body, through the soles of your feet.

You should now be able to begin to feel a surging of energy up through your feet.

Now come with me through the walk, through the roses on either side of you, and see how they turn towards you, as your thoughts go to them. They are aware of your appreciation of their beauty, of their colour, of their perfume. And as they collect your thoughts, so they in turn glow and radiate back to you, their Love, their happiness, at being able to give you the beauty, which they have to offer. This will continue throughout this path. Let us walk slowly and enjoy every moment of these roses, giving more life than you have ever seen in flowers.

And now feel the stems as you pass. There are no thorns, there's nothing to prevent your fingers touching the wood, and again, feeling the energy coming from these blooms.

Now let us continue through yet another archway, this time, with many hues of green. Imagine your country and the many shades of green, which appear to you in the spring. All those shades of green are encompassed in this one archway. And we go through there now, to the sound of falling water. Not falling water as you know it, but water singing the praise of the Creator, singing its happiness to give you the

Love, the colour, the sound, the music, which that water is emitting constantly.

And now, a surprise my friends, we shall walk through that waterfall, not behind it, not around it, through it. Come with me, step into the stream of water, which falls from above and walk through, through, through, not water, but a field of energy, which to you appears as water. Feel the energy surrounding you, permeating your bodies, blessing you, giving you happiness, giving you peace.

And now through the water and there is no rock formation behind, as you would expect upon your planet, but a vista of green fields, such as you have never seen. Those fields are amassed with what you would call 'wild' flowers, of every conceivable shape, hue, size, colour, perfume. Again, as you would describe upon this Earth, as a flowering meadow, but all those blooms, every blossom, is an individual point of energy. Again, you see the reason for discarding your footwear.

Let us walk through these plants. Do not worry you will not crush them. You will tread them down momentarily, but they will spring up, renewed as you pass. So have no fear of destroying any of them.

And now in such a field upon your Earth, would you not expect to find the nests of some types of your birds, who seek to live upon your Earth amongst the flowers and your vegetation? Look carefully and you should see some such amongst the flowers, wherein you now walk. Do not be afraid of stepping on any nest, you will not be able to do so, your feet will be guided around such nests. And note too that the parent birds do not fly in fear. As you approach, they watch you, but they remain with their nests and their fledglings. See if you can recognise any birds, such as are upon this Earth.

Now we will continue into the forest, which you see ahead. Again, not a forest that you would recognise as such. Many types of trees, many colours, many heights, some large, some small, but none being denied access to light and air—all growing vigorously, as is intended for them, all in harmony. Each one's colour blending with its neighbour. Now listen to the sound of the wind through the branches. Once more I say, not as you would hear it upon this Earth, but a wind, which sings with joy, as it caresses the branches, as it strokes the leaves with its breath, as it gives to those leaves the energy drawn from its cosmic birth and in return is given the energy from the soil, if you would call it that, in which the trees stand. When energy is given, another energy is taken, so life continues. It is given, it is taken, it is taken, it is given and the cycle is never-ending, never-ending. Listen to the laughter in that wind or breeze. Listen to it singing to you in welcome.

And as we go into this forest, though there are so many trees, you will become aware that nevertheless, there is no darkness, as you would expect. All is light, in spite of the thickness of the forest, in spite of the number of the trees. There is no shadow, there is no darkness, all is light, light, light. Look up above your heads and see what you would call the sunlight shining through, not between the leaves, but through the leaves—that is why there is no darkness, all is light, light, light.

And listen to the many little animals that live within this forest—none fearing, all happy, all contented with their place in the scheme of life. No death can come to them, as on this Earth, no fear can mark them. Listen to them.

Now let us continue. We come out of the forest, into a sandy plane. So far as you can see, there is apparently nothing growing, no living thing. Again listen, listen to the music that rises from that sand. Trilling, whistling, whispering, but all in harmony, all in harmony. And though it would appear that such land would be excessively hot, you do not feel it so under your feet. It is cool, pleasant, welcoming. Such is life within our sphere, always welcoming, always giving, always pleasant. Only your own thoughts can destroy what is there for you to enjoy.

And now we come to a large lake. You may have seen it shimmering in the sunlight. It is not blue, it is not green, it is a combination of all those shades of blue, all those shades of green, which you can imagine. And now another surprise for you my friends, we are going to walk across that water, not in it, but on it. Do not have fear. Follow me onto the water which will support you, unless you wish to be immersed in it, then you may do so. But no doubt it will be more exhilarating for you, to be able to walk upon the surface. Do you feel the energy, the warmth of the energy rising from this water? As I have said many times, all is energy, energy, energy.

And now, let us come to the far bank. And as we ascend from the water's edge, up to the field beyond, we go through many, many rushes, tall, waving, with no scent of decay, again as upon this Earth. There is no rotting of those unwanted—they are removed without the unpleasantness you experience here. As you go through, take some of those rushes in your hand. Feel the warmth, feel again the energy through your hand, into your arm, into your body. The purpose of this walk, was in the hope that you might, at each time I have spoken of it, feel the various energies, which exist and from which you cannot ever escape.

Pause

And now turn to this path on your left, and you will see in front of you, apparently a long way away, but in reality, quite near, a city of translucent buildings, gleaming, shining and again, welcoming. This is a city where all learning, all knowledge is gathered, for particular purposes. There are many such, many such, which in the gathering of their particular knowledge, feed other larger cities, where that knowledge is stored. But alas, I cannot take you into these buildings at this time. Let us walk past them. Feel the radiations from the walls as we pass—again energy, energy in colour, in light, in warmth, in welcome. And now my friends, we return to the gates. I will not tell you how, but you have encompassed a large area of land, without realising the last part of the journey was by thought, back to the entry. Here I leave you. I trust that my descriptions, my explanations, have been of help to you and have been of assistance, in enabling you to imagine, even if you did not experience the wealth of wonderment that awaits you, when you join us from your Earth.

I leave you now, to hopefully discuss your feelings with each other, to share each other's' experiences. And with my blessing.

I say goodbye to you all.

Printed in Great Britain
by Amazon

32809575R00169